50 simple ways to pamper your BABY

Karyn Siegel-Maier

STOREY
BOOKS

Schoolhouse Road
Pownal, Vermont 05261

Dedication

To mothers, fathers, and babies everywhere.
Special thanks to my parents and my children,
for all they have given me.

*The mission of Storey Communications is to serve our customers
by publishing practical information that encourages personal
independence in harmony with the environment.*

Edited by Deborah Balmuth and Robin Catalano
Cover design by Meredith Maker
Text design by Susan Bernier
Text production by Jennifer Jepson Smith
Cover and interior illustrations by Carleen Powell
Indexed by Nina Forrest, Looking Up Indexing Service

The information in this book is true and complete to the best of our
knowledge. All recommendations are made without guarantee on the part of
the author or Storey Books. The author and publisher disclaim any liability
in connection with the use of this information. For additional information
please contact Storey Books, Schoolhouse Road, Pownal, Vermont 05261.

Storey books are available for special premium and promotional uses and
for customized editions. For further information, please call Storey's Custom
Publishing Department at 1-800-793-9396.

Printed in the United States by R. R. Donnelley
10 9 8 7 6 5 4 3 2 1

Library of Congress Cataloging-in-Publication Data

Siegel-Maier, Karyn, 1960-
    50 simple ways to pamper your baby / Karyn Siegel-Maier
       p.   cm.
    Includes index.
    ISBN 1-58017-257-1 (pbk. : alk. paper)
    1. Infants (Newborn)—Care.   2. Infants—Care.   3. Parenting.
4. Child care.   I. Title: Fifty simple ways to pamper your baby.   II. Title.
  RG525.S5824   2000
  649'.122—dc21   99-086760
                                         CIP

Contents

Introduction

Parenting is one of the hardest tasks any person can undertake and one for which most of us feel the least prepared. First-time parents can easily feel overwhelmed with the never-ending responsibilities that accompany the arrival of a newborn. Even experienced parents encounter moments of exasperation and desperation. But, while parents are busy with the basics of caring for a baby, it's important for them to remember that their precious little one won't be little for long and that each step of the way, even the ordinary events that progress in a single day, represent a window of opportunity for growth.

Pampering a baby comes naturally — a kiss, a hug, or whispered words of tenderness flow easily from a loving parent. But in addition to these endearing expressions of affection, there are many more ways in which parents can positively impact the spirit and well-being of a developing child. And they can do so in ways that are in accord with the principles of natural living and simply having fun.

This book is not about childcare. There are volumes of books that will help you bear up through the difficulties of sibling rivalry, childhood diseases, and toilet training. What this book offers are various simple and common-sense ways in which you can nurture your child in the first year of life to provide the best foundation for wellness, self-esteem, and a lasting parental bond. The benefits that you both shall reap will endure a lifetime and become instilled in future generations.

As a parent, you naturally want the best for your baby. But the best gift you can give your child isn't a college education or annual vacations to Disneyland; it's the gift of yourself. This book will help you impart that gift freely in ways that may be new to you or in ways that you may never have considered.

Parenting is an adventure! Like a spin on the Ferris wheel, this life-long commitment will be filled with highs and lows. Enjoy the all-too-short ride.

INFORMATION AND CAUTIONS

All of the ingredients used in the formulas throughout this book can be found in many natural foods stores, in some supermarkets, and through mail-order suppliers. See Resources to help you locate and obtain various supplies and equipment.

Always measure all ingredients carefully and keep them stored away from children and pets. Essential oils are highly concentrated and should always be handled with particular caution. Do not use essential oils undiluted unless specified or in amounts greater than recommended, and never use them internally. Should any rash, redness, or other skin irritation develop after using any formula or ingredient, discontinue its use and seek the advice of a qualified health care practitioner.

Make the Most of Your Time

Pampering your baby truly begins in the womb, so giving yourself a little extra attention during this special time is important right from the start. One way to do this is to take back control of the time you give to others.

Time's on Your Side

During your pregnancy, be sure to take time out to be "alone" — just you and baby. Getting away from ringing phones and the daily grind for a few minutes each day will do wonders for both of you. Try to find a serene place, such as a garden or a quiet nook in your home, where you won't be disturbed. Close your eyes, push away all "things to do" thoughts, and take a few deep breaths. Without speaking, communicate thoughts of love to your unborn child.

Learn to say "no." Your energy is precious, and you can't afford to give it away, especially during those times when you feel you have none to give! Gently but firmly inform the people who place unnecessary demands on your time that the world will not come to an end if you are unable to comply with their requests.

Delegate tasks to others. Unless you operate by contract in your home, duties such as laundry and food shopping are not exclusively your domain. Ask other family members to pitch in; even young children can put away groceries or prepare a salad. And, when help is offered without your encouragement, take it!

Take time to record your thoughts and feelings. This is a great time to start a journal; if you already have a journal or diary, start a special section devoted to your pregnancy. Another great way to preserve your feelings during this time is to write letters to your unborn child. Commit a little time each day to writing down whatever comes to mind; having this time scheduled might give you the excuse you need to take a time-out.

A Womb-ful of Sound

The womb is hardly a quiet place. The fetus constantly perceives digestive sounds, heart rhythms, and external noises. In fact, the usual noise level inside the womb is equivalent to that within an average-sized apartment! And there is increasing evidence that, after birth, babies can recognize certain voices, songs, and stories they repeatedly heard in the womb. Since baby is already learning about the outside world from the sounds she hears, why not give her something of interest to listen to?

Music to Little Ears

Sing to your baby while walking, working around the house, or just sitting quietly. I sang the same song every day while I was pregnant and then for many years after birth at bedtime.

Read some of your favorite poems or short stories out loud. If you have other children, invite them to sing or read along with you.

Give your developing baby the gift of music. Unborn babies don't really prefer one style of music over another. So, if you find jazz or rock and roll more soothing than classical, play on!

Attend a musical event. If you enjoy concerts and recitals, introduce them to baby now! You'll both find the music stimulating and relaxing.

A WORD OF CAUTION

It isn't necessary to direct loud noises at the mother's abdomen to get baby's attention. In fact, doing so could be harmful. Sound passes easily through amniotic fluid, and studies show that loud noises may cause the baby to urinate, indicating sensitivity to sudden sounds.

Reduce Stress, Increase Energy

It's no secret that your body's demands during pregnancy can lead to fatigue. During this time, everyday stress can take a toll on your and your baby's health and well-being. You might be surprised to find that it's not the big stuff that can wear you down, like a change of residence or preparing to leave your job; it's the accumulated total of all the little things that you face every day, like household chores, financial responsibilities, and wondering if you'll ever have a waistline again. When you find yourself sweating the small stuff, try these easy stress reducers.

Relaxation Therapy

Not only do regular walks help to bring you back into psychological balance, but also the exercise will benefit both you and your baby. If possible, walk in natural environments such as parks or a wooded path.

Meditate with relaxation tapes or soothing instrumental music. Take a moment to clear your mind and relax your body. With your eyes closed, take in long, deep breaths through your mouth; then exhale slowly through your nostrils. As you exhale, concentrate on a single thought or image; try repeating a single word to yourself (such as "one") or imagining that you can "see" through your forehead.

Take a load off your tired feet. And, while you're at it, why not treat yourself to an herbal foot soak? To a small plastic tub of warm water, add 3 to 6 drops of lavender essential oil or ¼ cup of fresh lavender flowers. You can also add several small, round pebbles to the tub and massage your feet over them while you soak.

Need a quick fix for stress? Just place 1 drop of lavender or rose essential oil on a tissue or cotton cloth and inhale when needed. A scented hankie travels well too. See the box on page 9 for more information on using essential oils.

Give yourself a soothing facial massage. Combine 1 teaspoon of sweet almond oil or jojoba oil with 1 drop of chamomile or lavender essential oil and blend well. Using your fingertips, massage the mixture around your temples, jaw line, cheekbones, and brow line.

Aromatherapy for Balance

These formulas are intended to be inhaled, not applied to the skin. (Note: Most experts recommend that essential oils not be used during the first three months of pregnancy.)

> **For emotional/mental stress:** I drop each of bergamot, sandalwood, and geranium essential oils.
> **For fatigue:** I drop each of rosemary, chamomile, and lavender essential oils.
> **To beat the "blues":** I drop each of nutmeg, lemon, and frankincense essential oils.
> **For muscle aches:** I drop each of chamomile, geranium, and jasmine essential oils.
> **For nausea:** I drop each of fennel, coriander, and cardamom essential oils.
> **To calm:** I drop each of cedar, sweet orange, and chamomile essential oils.
> **To stimulate:** I drop each of eucalyptus, lemon, and rosemary essential oils.

Put sweet almond oil (which has no fragrance) in a small glass bottle; add desired essential oil blend.

To use: place a few drops of the blended oil on a soft cloth and inhale as needed.

4

Mother the Mother

With so much focus on the new arrival, it's easy to forget to take care of your personal needs. But feeling good is just as important as preparing for the delivery. The better you feel, the more at ease you'll be when tending to your little one.

Be Good to Yourself

Pregnancy is a wonderful time, but you'll no doubt experience occasional discomfort. These easy, do-it-yourself treatments will help soothe pregnancy-related aches and pains.

Stretch Mark Reducer: Blend together 2 ounces of sweet almond oil, 1 ounce of wheat germ oil, 8 drops of borage seed oil, 6 drops of carrot essential oil, and 3 drops of rose essential oil. Lightly massage onto the breasts, buttocks, and thighs once daily.

Varicose Vein Therapy: Blend together 1 ounce of carrier oil (such as avocado or sweet almond), 4 drops of geranium essential oil, and 2 drops of cypress essential oil. Lightly massage the oil into the legs, working from the ankle to the thigh. (*Note:* Some women should not massage varicose veins due to other complications. Check with your doctor first.)

Breast Workout: To 1 ounce of sweet almond oil, add 3 drops each of clary sage, carrot, and geranium essential oils; blend well. Apply the oil with circular motions, starting at the center of the breast and moving outward to the armpit. This formula is helpful during the last trimester of pregnancy when the breasts are actively preparing for milk production. To help prepare the nipples for nursing, roll them between the thumb and forefinger with increasing regularity and pressure.

Hemorrhoid Help: Blend 4 drops of carrier oil with 1 drop of cypress essential oil and 2 drops of myrrh essential oil. Spread the mixture around the anal area to relieve discomfort as needed.

Get the Support You Need

We all know why bringing a baby into the world is called *labor,* but there's actually quite a bit of work to do before the "main event." All expecting parents, especially first-time ones, need plenty of support from a variety of caregivers. Here are some suggestions for finding the right champions to make your birth experience the most positive it can be.

It Takes Teamwork

Get acquainted with a doula. While the word might sound like an exotic pastry, this Greek term actually means "woman caretaker." A doula is a professional childbirth assistant who works side by side with your birth partner (your husband, midwife, or labor coach) to provide additional emotional and physical support throughout your pregnancy and delivery. For more information on finding a qualified doula, see Resources.

Consider a birthing center. Birthing centers differ from hospitals in that they offer a less clinical environment and approach to care. Many hospitals now offer natural birthing classes and programs as well. Some communities also have women's health centers with staff midwives and physicians who will help you prepare for giving birth at home. Your physician or midwife can give you more information about facilities and programs in your area.

Consult with a nutrition expert. You're eating for two, and since everything you eat and drink at this time is filtered through your baby, it's important to get all the vitamins and minerals you both need. A nutritionist or dietician can help you plan meals made from fresh, whole foods (organic, ideally) that will meet all your nutritional requirements while minimizing excessive weight gain.

In motherhood, there's so much to learn, so much to give, and although the learning gets less with each succeeding child, the giving never does.

— Marguerite Kelly

The Joy of Prenatal Massage

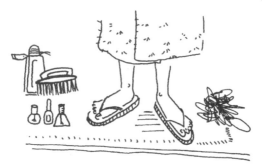

Prenatal massage offers many benefits. Perhaps most importantly, it fosters a feeling of connection with the baby for the mother and the partner giving the massage. Prenatal massage also reduces stress and fatigue, improves muscle tone, and encourages the elimination of toxins.

Note: Get the "okay" from your doctor before embarking on a full body massage. In addition, natal "kneads" of the mother's abdomen should be performed only by a trained massage therapist and only after the first trimester. Improper massage work on the abdomen can be detrimental, so limit self-massage or a massage given by a partner to the back, neck, shoulders, hands, and feet. A belly rub of very light pressure is also acceptable.

Ah, There's the Rub!

The Belly Rub: With the mother lying on her back, very gently and slowly glide the palm of your hand over her belly in a circular, clockwise motion. (This also aids digestion.) Use only light pressure. Don't be surprised if the baby responds to your touch and begins to follow your trail!

HEAVENLY HOMEMADE MASSAGE OILS

You can make your own all-natural massage formulas from readily available carrier and essential oils. *Note:* Never exceed the recommended dosages of essential oils. Certain essential oils should be avoided altogether during pregnancy. These include: pennyroyal, tansy, peppermint, wintergreen, licorice, juniper, cohosh, and rue. In addition, most experts recommend that all essential oils not be used during the first three months of pregnancy.

Basic Massage Oil: In 1 ounce of sweet almond oil, blend 2 drops of lavender essential oil and 1 drop of chamomile essential oil. Or, if you prefer a more earthy scent, use 2 drops of patchouli essential oil and 1 drop of neroli essential oil.

Best Belly Massage Oil: In 1 ounce of sweet almond oil, blend the contents of 1 vitamin E capsule and 1 drop each of rose, lavender, and chamomile essential oils.

Neck, Shoulders, and Back: These are areas where tension lives, in the form of taut muscles. With the mother sitting upright, massage these areas with gentle, circular motions using both the fingertips and the palms of the hands. Be careful not to pull or roll the skin — mother's skin is already stretched to the limit!

Hands and Feet: It's remarkable how relaxing a massage of the hands and feet can feel. Pay special attention to the arch of the foot and the knuckles and joints of the fingers. Consult a book on reflexology and acupressure to get the most benefit.

BASIC MASSAGE MOVEMENTS

Swedish massage is the most widely used form of massage in the Western world and incorporates five basic techniques:

- Effleurage — long, gliding movements with flattened hands.
- Friction — deep circular motions with the thumbs and fingertips.
- Petrissage — gently lifting and kneading muscles.
- Vibration — rapidly moving muscles back and forth for a few seconds with a flattened hand.
- Tapotement — tapping and chopping movements to increase muscle energy.

7

Welcome Baby

Well, the long-anticipated day has finally arrived, and with it, one of the miracles of your life — your child. The first moments and days after baby's birth are very precious indeed; here are several ways to make this time and transition more special for everyone.

Precious Moments

Try to keep your baby in your hospital room or bedroom instead of the nursery as much as possible. You both have a lot to learn about each other.

Name that baby! There are many good books that can help you select an appropriate name for your baby. Choose carefully — it's an imprint that will last for life. You can even hold your own naming ceremony or craft homemade announcements to tell your loved ones about the new arrival.

Start a daily journal, or continue writing in the diary you started during your pregnancy. You'll be up at rather odd times during the night, so you might as well put to good use those moments when you're not nursing. A journal of your thoughts and feelings at this time will be something very special to share with your child years from now. My tattered journal still gets pulled from the bookshelf now and then.

Save those cards and letters! You're sure to receive lots of "welcome baby" cards upon baby's arrival. Put them in a keepsake box and share them with your child when she's old enough to be curious about the day she was born.

In the sheltered simplicity of the first days after a baby is born, one sees again the magical closed circle, the miraculous sense of two people existing only for each other.

— Anne Morrow Lindbergh

Limit your visitors. Newborns have underdeveloped immune systems and can easily catch colds from a well-meaning friend or relative. Try to limit visitors to immediate family for the first few weeks. There will be plenty of time to introduce the rest of the world to your baby later on.

Take lots of pictures (but avoid using the flash). Dad is usually very happy to take on this task!

Power up your video camera. You can capture your baby's first moments of life to share with those closest to you later. Many people record the birth event itself.

Celebrate the gift of life. Consider inviting your parents, your in-laws, or your other children (if they're old enough) to the birth event. And, while all are gathered near, get a group picture taken or capture all the generations on videotape.

Surround Your Baby with Softness

Babies come into the world with tender new skin that's as soft and delicate as . . . well, a baby's bottom! Shouldn't their surroundings be just as soft?

Put Your Angel on a Cloud

Sling your baby. This over-the-shoulder baby holder is an ancient device that plays an important role in "attachment" parenting — a philosophy of maintaining maximum physical closeness as well as responsiveness and sensitivity to baby's needs. Research shows that regular "baby wearing" reduces daytime crying by 43 percent and night-time crying by 51 percent. In addition, babies frequently carried in a sling spend more time in a "quiet-alert state," which promotes learning, coping ability, and bonding with parents. Choose a sling made of good quality organic cotton or hemp.

Wrap your baby in an all-natural blanket. Several companies make baby blankets of either 100 percent cotton or lamb's wool. They last for years and provide soft comfort without the use of synthetic fibers or cotton grown with pesticides.

The bedding you choose for your baby's crib is important, too. Choose bumpers, mattress pads, and pillows (for older babies) made of and filled with cotton; not only are they more comfortable than synthetic items but they're also more durable and free of chemical residues. A mattress made of organic materials is a good idea also. (For information on ordering these items, see Resources.)

Dress your baby in natural, organic fibers. Natural clothing is soft, free of toxic chemicals and dyes, and available in beautiful, lush earth tones.

Cloth diapers are the best for your baby. Cotton allows your baby's skin to breathe and reduces painful diaper rash.

Build a Better Nest

Just as you would avoid feeding your baby harmful substances, you will want to limit her exposure to environmental toxins. Furniture, paints, and other materials can emit potentially harmful chemicals without your even knowing it. In fact, the pollutant level inside the average home is much greater than that of outdoor air! By using nontoxic materials, you can make the nursery a safe place as well as a cozy haven.

The Natural Nursery

Color your baby's world with natural paints, pigments, and stains. Nearly 10 percent of the airborne pollutants in the home come from volatile organic compounds (VOCs) in paint. Many of the larger paint manufacturers now produce low-VOC paints, and several companies produce natural paint alternatives, such as casein or milk paint, in a variety of rich colors. These paints are not only VOC-free but the oldest and most durable form of paint known. In fact, milk paint has been found on decorative pieces buried in King Tut's tomb! (See Resources.)

Garage sales and auctions are great places to find unusual pieces of furniture for the nursery. But if you plan to invest in used furniture or use hand-me-downs, you'll need to check all parts and hardware for wear that could cause injury. You might also want to remove the finish and use a natural paint or stain and a nontoxic sealant.

A futon in the nursery? Sure! Futons aren't just for adults anymore. Several companies manufacture crib futons made from all-natural, nontoxic materials. For newborns, "Moses-style" woven baskets are also available as an alternative to traditional bassinets. (See Resources for more information.)

Create a dreamy wall or ceiling mural with clouds, stars, suns, and moons! Such fantasy works of art will not only soothe and entertain your baby, but spark his creative imagination, too.

There are other earth-friendly products and accessories that you can use to reduce toxicity in the home, such as natural flooring and carpeting made from recycled soda bottles. For sources for these products, see Resources.

Nontoxic, Do-It-Yourself Paint

This paint spreads easily and imparts rich color tones while still allowing wood to breathe. Use it on wood furniture, doors, moldings, and window frames. You can also use this paint on dry wall or other absorbent surfaces.

- 3 cups turpentine (this ingredient is made from pine resin and is nontoxic)
- 1 cup linseed oil
- 5–6 tablespoons mineral pigment (see Resources)
- 2 tablespoons drying agent (see Resources)

Mix all ingredients together until well blended. With a soft cloth or natural-bristle brush, apply paint to a prepared wall or wood surface and allow to penetrate for 30 minutes. Wipe off excess. For deeper color, repeat these steps as many times as you wish. When the paint is completely dry, coat the surface with a nontoxic sealant if desired.

Making Scents for Baby

Smell is the only sense fully developed in humans at birth. It's little wonder, then, that babies respond quite readily to aromatherapy. A diffuser comes in handy when using essential oils for aromatherapy, but keep in mind that essential oils should never be used "neat" (undiluted) in a diffuser in a baby's room. Their concentration is too strong for little lungs. Instead, dilute the essential oil in a base oil, such as jojoba or sweet almond.

Scents-Abilities

Here's the simplest way to use aromatherapy in a small baby's nursery: Add the essential oils to water in a simmer pot or even to a small pan of warm water (about 1½ cups); place the pot or pan in the room out of the reach of baby, siblings, and pets. The following combinations are especially soothing. (If you're using a diffuser, dilute the essential oils in 2 tablespoons of base oil.)

Nursing Aide: For a very relaxing, pleasant atmosphere to enjoy while quietly nursing your baby, add 1 drop each of chamomile, dill, and sweet orange essential oils to the pan or simmer pot.

Stuffy Nose Relief: Place 1 drop of lemon essential oil and 2 drops of eucalyptus essential oil in the pan or simmer pot.

Sleepy Time Formula: Place 1 drop each of chamomile and dill essential oils in the pan or simmer pot.

I think it must be somewhere written, that the virtues of mothers shall be visited on their children.

— Charles Dickens

Guide to Using Essential Oils
for Aromatherapy

Age	Amount
Under 2 months	1–3 drops, diluted
2–12 months	3–5 drops, diluted
1–2 years	5–10 drops, diluted

The essential oils listed below are gentle and safe for use around babies and young children. Please remember that essential oils are highly concentrated and should always be used diluted, whether in a diffuser or on the skin. Also, just a reminder: Essential oils should never be used internally.

- Calendula — a natural deodorizer
- Chamomile — soothing, improves a variety of skin conditions
- Dill — has a calming effect and is traditionally used to induce sleep in babies
- Lavender — relaxing, has antiviral and anti-inflammatory properties
- Mandarin — invigorating, reduces tension
- Neroli — enhances mood, has mild sedative effects
- Rose otto — relaxing, enhances mood
- Sweet orange — a natural antiseptic, soothing
- Yarrow — has astringent qualities, reduces inflammation

Follow the Road to Confidence

Babies don't come into the world with blueprints or an owner's manual of operation. But, incredibly, your baby does come equipped with built-in mechanisms to tell you when something is wrong or when everything is right with her world — signals generally recognized as crying and cooing.

"In Me I Trust!"

What's even more amazing is that everyone else seems to know what's best for your baby, even better than you do. People love to give advice when it comes to a complicated "device" such as an infant.

But sometimes too much information can leave you feeling inept, as though you're doing everything wrong. How can you keep your sanity during these times? By trusting yourself.

Don't even think about trying to do it all! For the first several weeks, babies have their own ideas about when they should eat and sleep — and if you try to get baby to adapt to *your* schedule, you might find yourself forgetting simple things like your social security number. So, when baby is resting, you should be, too. Believe me, the dirt on the kitchen floor will still be there later. (And, don't let other people's negative opinions of your housekeeping get under your skin!)

Follow your instincts. It's a universal truth: What you don't already know about caring for babies, your baby will teach you in short order.

Listen to advice and then treat it like an old sweater. If it fits, wear it; if it doesn't, don't.

Let your cup overflow. Cuddling your baby is a healthy way of nurturing him both emotionally and physically. Pooh-pooh anyone who tries to convince you that you'll spoil your baby if you pick him up too often.

Establish a network with other new parents. The couples you met during childbirth classes are the very folks going through the same trials as you; just sharing your day-to-day concerns and joys can be enough to get you through the rough spots.

Don't cry over spilt milk. Accept the fact that you'll make mistakes in the beginning. If you feel you can't yet flawlessly change a diaper or burp a baby, rest assured that you'll get better at it in time. Practice, after all, makes perfect.

Read as much information as you can. Today's style of parenting might differ greatly from your parents', and it's up to *you* to decide what's best for your baby. There are several excellent publications and magazines dedicated to providing sensible and reliable information. (See Resources for suggestions.)

The more people have studied different methods of bringing up children, the more they have come to the conclusion that what good mothers and fathers instinctively feel like doing for their babies is the best after all.

— Benjamin Spock

12

A Delicate Area

Whon you think about it, the umbilical cord is an amazing thing. When my youngest was born, I was fascinated by its construction and the idea that we once shared the same heartbeat. But once the cord is cut and tied after birth, it looks a lot less interesting as it shrivels on your baby's belly on its way to becoming a navel.

For the most part, mother nature takes care of this process herself; don't do anything to treat it for at least 24 hours. But, since infection is a possibility, you'll want to keep the area dry and free of bacteria in the days that follow until the final remains of the cord wither and drop off, usually within seven to ten days.

Help in Healing

Make an herbal antiseptic powder. Combine ¼ cup of pure cornstarch (or arrowroot powder) and 2 teaspoons of pure, ground thyme. After bathing and drying baby's skin, dust the area around the cord with a cotton ball dipped in this powder. (*Note:* Always shield baby's face to prevent inhalation of powders.)

Give it the lavender treatment. Lavender is known for its antibacterial properties and its ability to speed the healing of skin. In a small cup, mix 1 tablespoon of pure water with 1 drop of lavender essential oil. Dip a cotton ball into the lavender mixture and gently clean the area around the umbilical cord.

Flaky, dry skin around the umbilical cord can be soothed with this formula. Combine 2 tablespoons of sweet almond oil, 3 drops of German chamomile essential oil, and 1 drop of rose essential oil. Massage 2–3 drops of this mixture into skin around the cord twice daily. Incidentally, this formula can also be used to help improve irregular skin pigmentation on other parts of the body. (*Note:* Birthmarks will fade only with time, if at all.)

The Disappearing Cradle Cap Trick

Cradle cap is not a disease but actually a sign of healthy skin growth. In adults, new skin cells are generated at about the same rate as old ones die and are shed. But in infants, new skin cells often grow at a faster rate than the old, creating these telltale greasy, scaly patches.

Give It the Brush-Off

Cradle cap is very common, but it's rather unsightly when it comes off in large clumps or layers. And although your baby can't tell you directly if it feels uncomfortable, it seems likely that it could be itchy. Here are some simple ways to alleviate this bothersome condition.

To help soften cradle cap, massage in a few drops of this infused oil before shampooing: Blend 2 tablespoons of sweet almond oil with 1 drop each of calendula and geranium essential oils. For best results, use this formula once each day, taking care around the fontanelle, or "soft spot," until all of the secretions disappear.

Cocoa Butter and Slippery Elm Formula

This formula is simple to make and has a relatively long shelf life. Slippery elm bark is high in mucilage, which will help to loosen cradle cap's grip on the scalp.

- ¼ cup sweet almond oil
- 2 tablespoons powdered slippery elm bark
- 1 tablespoon pure cocoa butter

1. In a nonstick saucepan over low heat, gently heat the sweet almond oil and powdered slippery elm bark for 5–10 minutes, until warm and mixed well. Add cocoa butter; stirring constantly, heat 5 minutes longer.

2. Strain the mixture through a mesh strainer into a short, widemouthed jar; let stand until cool. Refrigerate until the mixture is completely solid; then store in a cool, dry place.

3. Apply the solid paste with your fingertips to affected areas before shampooing, gently rubbing with a washcloth or soft brush to loosen crusty patches. Discard any unused portion after 6 weeks.

A natural after-shampoo rinse made from a cooled infusion of comfrey is also helpful. Bring 1 quart of water and 1½ ounces of sliced dried comfrey root to a boil. Simmer for 20 to 30 minutes; then strain, reserving the liquid. Apply to the area using a washcloth, gently loosening crusty patches. This rinse will keep in the refrigerator for up to 1 week, but let it sit out for a few hours to return to room temperature before using.

A soft, natural-bristle brush is not only good for a young baby's hair (if she has any!), but also helpful for loosening and removing cradle cap.

Using a 100-percent cotton washcloth on your baby's scalp while bathing will also help to loosen and remove crusty spots. Be sure to rinse the hair thoroughly to remove any small particles of cradle cap that may remain trapped in the hair.

Have Fun in the Tub

Bathtime is a fun time for both parent and baby! Just make sure the room is warm and free of drafts, and gather everything you'll need before you get started.

Rub-a-Dub-Dub

Consider installing a water filter to make sure your bathing (and drinking) water is as pure as it can be.

Instead of using a washcloth, invest in a large cellulite sponge. They're soft and squishy (adding to the fun value), and they last a long time.

A soft, 100-percent cotton hooded towel is great for wrapping up baby when the splishing and splashing is over. It's a perfect way to keep baby warm and cozy while you snuggle up for a story, to nurse, or to take a nap together.

Babies three months or older will enjoy a bath with mom or dad. Just make sure the water temperature is adjusted for baby's tender skin, not yours, and take care to keep baby's head above water level.

Talk, sing, or recite poetry to your baby while bathing her. Even if no one else appreciates your oratory talents, your baby will be captivated by the rhythm of your voice, especially when it's combined with your soothing touch.

Condition your baby's skin with an infused herbal oil. Blend 1 teaspoon of sweet almond oil or hazelnut oil with 1 drop of chamomile, lavender, or yarrow essential oil and add to baby's bath water, dispersing well with your fingers.

Herbal baths are relaxing and therapeutic. To a full tub of warm water, add 1 (and only 1) drop of one of the following essential oils: lavender, chamomile, yarrow, or geranium. Make sure you distribute the oil in the water with your fingers before putting your baby in the tub. Alternately, you can add the essential oil to ½ cup of milk (a great softening agent!) or use ½ cup of cooled herbal tea in place of the essential oil.

Herbal Bath Bag

Bath bags are one of the easiest and most inexpensive herbal preparations you can make. To make your bath bags, you'll need fresh or dried herbs that you've either grown yourself or purchased from a reliable natural foods store. Herbal baths are so soothing you'll want to use this recipe for yourself!

> 1 medium square of cotton cloth (about the size of a washcloth)
> 2 tablespoons fresh or dried lavender, chamomile, lemon balm, calendula, yarrow, or dill (or a combination of several)
> 1 6- to 8-inch length of ribbon or string

1. Place the herbs in the center of the cloth; bring the corners up to the center to form a bag. Firmly secure the top with the ribbon or string.

2. Place the bath bag in a tub of warm water. Let the herbs infuse in the bath water for at least 5 minutes. Remove the bag before placing the baby in the tub.

Perhaps the best thing about the future is that it only comes one day at a time.

— Dean Acheson

Bottoms Up!

Diaper rash feels as painful to your baby as it looks to you. Frequent diaper changes are necessary to prevent a rash from getting a foothold. But avoid using petroleum-based creams; though they might form an effective barrier from moisture, they aren't good for your baby's skin. Instead, try these natural methods for preventing and treating diaper rash.

Skin Savers

This is a great alternative to commercial baby wipes. Fill a sterilized widemouthed canning jar with a solution of 1 cup of water, 2 drops of lavender essential oil, and 1 drop of chamomile essential oil. Add multiple folded squares of pure cotton or cellulite to the jar. Shake well and store at room temperature. To use, remove a cloth, squeeze out any excess liquid, and gently wipe over baby's skin. Wash and reuse these wipes whenever possible.

For older babies, sunshine is one of the best cures for diaper rash. Weather permitting, let your little one expose her bum to the early-morning or late-afternoon sun. Make sure you apply a sunscreen first and limit the exposure time to about 10 minutes to prevent sunburn! (See page 55.)

Diaper Rash Prevention Cream

½ cup 100% pure aloe vera gel
½ cup cocoa butter
2 tablespoons jojoba or sweet almond oil
contents of 3 vitamin E capsules
6 drops calendula essential oil

1. In a small saucepan, combine the aloe vera gel, cocoa butter, and jojoba or sweet almond oil. Heat on very low heat, stirring constantly, until the cocoa butter is completely melted. Stir in the contents of the vitamin E capsules and mix well.

2. Remove from heat and let cool for 5 minutes; then stir again. Blend in the calendula essential oil.

3. Pour the mixture into small sterile glass jars and let cool completely before capping. Needs no refrigeration.

Planes, Trains, and Teethers

Recent reports have warned that certain materials used in making baby bottles, teethers, and soft plastic toys, especially those designed to make their way to a baby's mouth, may present certain risks to children. Of main concern is polyvinyl chloride (PVC), otherwise known as vinyl, as well as a phthalate dubbed DINP. These chemicals can be absorbed from certain teethers and toys and have even been found to leach into infant formula from plastic bottles. Studies have linked these agents with liver damage and cancer. To be sure your baby is completely safe, you'll want to avoid these materials.

Buy Wisely

Shop at one of the major stores that claim to reject phthalate-based baby products. According to a recent issue of *Consumer Reports,* these include Wal-Mart, Sears, Kmart, Toys "R" Us, and Target. (*Note:* This policy does not necessarily apply to children's toys.)

Replace shiny "plastic" bottles (their packaging does not always specify what they're actually made of) with glass bottles or those made from a dull, opaque plastic. The latter are often colored and made from polyethylene and do not leach bisphenol-A, another questionable component.

Opt for toys made from wood or cloth instead of plastic. The Internet is a wonderful source for craftspeople and hobbyists who make and sell old-fashioned wooden or fabric toys. You'll also find listings for companies offering "natural" baby products, including toys and stuffed animals made without dyes or other irritants. See Resources for more about natural toys.

Get involved with organizations that campaign for the manufacturing of phthalate-free toys and baby products, such as the Children's Environmental Coalition or Greenpeace. (See Resources for contact information.)

If plastic toys do make their way into your life, make sure they're made from nonchlorinated plastics labeled as polyethylene 2 or 4, or polypropylene 5. If in doubt, call the manufacturer.

Make a statement to manufacturers and hold them liable for their actions. Ship their PVC toys back to them.

MAKE-YOUR-OWN PLAYTHINGS

Safe and creative playthings for baby can be quickly assembled from ordinary household items. Plastic bowls and wooden spoons from the kitchen will inspire your little drummer. Older babies will enjoy stacking various sized bowls and cups.

PVC-free plastic cups, bottles, or bowls can entertain and teach at bath time, too. Baby will enjoy filling such items with water and spilling the water out again. This activity is especially fun if you poke a hole or two in the bottom of the plastic item.

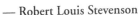

I will make you brooches and toys for your delight
Of birdsong at morning and starshine at night.

— Robert Louis Stevenson

Introducing...
Leonardo daBaby!

At nine months of age, a baby is ready to explore the world of art. But be forewarned: Constant supervision and, at times, an art smock and plenty of towels are necessary to observe safely and preserve your furnishings. Keep soap and water nearby, too.

Artistic Endeavors

The next time you sit down to write a letter or pay bills, offer baby a large sheet of paper and a single super-sized, nontoxic crayon. At first he'll stab at the paper, but soon he'll begin to mimic your motions. Supervision is required!

Let your baby finger-food paint! Spread out some waxed paper on her high chair tray and offer pudding, mashed potatoes, or oatmeal as edible, no-worry finger paints.

Make stickers out of nontoxic materials and show your older baby how to create mosaic art with them. Using nontoxic paper and markers, draw your sticker designs. Cut out the shapes and brush the backs of them with a mixture of 1 package of any flavor gelatin and 2 tablespoons of *boiling* water. Let the "glue" dry. When licked, the shapes stick to cardboard or paper.

Homespun Play Clay

Get into baby sculpture! Forget modeling clays and "doughs" that can be toxic or may stain fabrics. Using nontoxic ingredients, you can make your own mixtures that are just as fun and colorful.

> 1 cup flour
> 1 cup water
> ½ cup salt
> 1 tablespoon vegetable oil
> 2 teaspoons cream of tartar
> food coloring of choice

1. Combine all ingredients in a heavy, nonstick saucepan; mix well. Heat slowly over low, stirring constantly.

2. When the mixture forms a ball, turn it onto a clean surface and knead until smooth and elastic. Let cool completely. Store in an airtight container. Refrigerate for up to 2 weeks.

If you have a personal computer, look for shareware or buy software that lets baby make artistic designs. These programs are usually geared for babies 18 months or older and are referred to as "lapware," since a parental lap is usually required.

Nontoxic Finger Paint

If your baby ends up with this homemade "paint" on her face, you won't have to worry about how safe it is. And it washes off easily!

1 ½ cups cold water
1 cup flour
2 tablespoons salt
1 ¼ cups hot water
assorted food colorings

1. In a heavy saucepan over low to medium heat, combine cold water, flour, and salt. Using a whisk or rotary beater, beat until a smooth paste forms. Add hot water; boil until mixture thickens.

2. Remove the pan from heat. Add food coloring and beat again until smooth. Refrigerate unused portions for up to 2 weeks.

Let Your Powders Be Natural

Talcum powder, or talc, is a common ingredient in body powders, but it's not the best to use on your baby. Talc is extremely fine; it's easily inhaled and can lead to chemical pneumonia. It can also contain minute traces of arsenic. Better choices for making simple, absorbent powders for your baby include cornstarch, arrowroot powder, French clay, rice flour, and powdered herbal flowers such as elder, chamomile, lavender, and calendula.

O young thing, your mother's lovely armful! How sweet the fragrance of your body!

— Euripides

Pamper with Powder

Commercial baby powders can include other questionable ingredients, including synthetic fragrances that can cause irritation. Once again, simple ingredients can replace those that nature didn't intend for your baby.

When using powders on your baby, always shield her face to prevent accidental inhalation. In fact, it's a good idea to put the powder in your hand before powdering her bottom.

Healing Baby Powder

The lavender essential oil used in the formula will reduce redness and inflammation caused by skin irritations and prevent the occurrence of diaper rash. (Note: This powder is also an excellent one for parents to use during warm weather on areas such as underarms and feet.)

- 2 cups cornstarch
- 2 cups arrowroot powder
- 3 tablespoons French clay
- ½ cup powdered calendula flowers
- 6 drops lavender essential oil

In a large mixing bowl, blend the cornstarch, arrowroot powder, French clay, and calendula flowers. Sprinkle the essential oil into the mixture and blend well. Store the finished powder in tins, short glass jars, or plastic containers with shaker tops.

Silky Baby Blend

This formula will protect baby's skin from excess moisture and leave it feeling silky smooth. The addition of aloe vera powder (available in health food stores and by mail order) speeds healing of minor skin irritations. The chamomile and lavender essential oils work together to produce a calming effect, as well.

- 3 cups cornstarch
- 2 cups French clay
- ½ cup aloe vera powder
- ½ cup powdered lavender flowers
- 4 drops chamomile essential oil
- 2 drops lavender essential oil

In a large mixing bowl, blend cornstarch, French clay, aloe vera powder, and lavender flowers. Sprinkle the essential oils into the mixture and blend well. Store the powder in tins, short glass jars, or plastic containers with shaker tops.

19

Get Down and Goofy

Babies love to laugh, especially at you. And babies have an uncanny way of reducing even the most reserved adult to a walking tower of gurgles, "goo-goos," and guffaws. Here are a few time-tested ways to elicit a hearty chuckle from your little one.

Make 'em Laugh!

Talk silly. Don't underestimate the power of total nonsense! Sing a crazy song of your own creation, with lots of rhyming words and gibberish. Soon you'll be laughing too, which will only add to baby's glee.

This one may soon tire mom or dad, but baby will enjoy this trick over and over. Fill a small clean spray bottle with cool water. Lightly spritz baby's bare feet when she isn't looking.

Tear it up! Believe it or not, many six- to nine-month-old babies delight in watching you perform the simple act of tearing up strips of paper. (Don't forget to recycle them when you're finished.)

Try the bumblebee surprise. Raise your hand with one finger extended and slowly make your way down to baby's belly, spiraling as you go and making a "z-z-z" sound. When you've reached your target, move in for the "sting" by gently poking his belly.

Give the old Bronx cheer! With baby lying on her back, press your lips to her belly and gently blow through your lips to make them vibrate. (*Note:* This works best on a bare belly.)

Here's one where you can really use your noodle. Let a long strand of linguini or spaghetti dangle from your mouth. Then, with baby watching, slowly suck it into your mouth until it disappears. If you can make the noodle slap from side to side, so much the better.

Where's baby's nose? Ask that question as you pretend to swipe baby's nose. Announce that you have it while presenting your thumb between your middle and forefinger to imitate his captured nose. As baby catches on, he'll begin to swipe your nose in turn. But don't be surprised if he doesn't give it back. My son once took mine and then proceeded to "swallow" it, announcing that it was "aw gone!"

Baby will find hilarity in the classic bubbles-through-the-straw game. Fill a glass half full of water; then immerse a straw in the water and blow through it. (*Note:* Baby will eventually learn to imitate this trick and will likely continue this behavior right through junior high school.)

Take baby on a magic carpet ride. Lay her face down on a blanket, rug, or towel, and then drag her around the room by pulling on the blanket. Pre-walking babies find this a very amusing way to get around. (*Note:* Baby should be at least six months old to do this trick.)

Mother, let us imagine we are traveling, and passing through a strange and dangerous country.

— Rabindranath Tagore

Build a Strong Bond

Two of the most important gifts you will ever give your child are a feeling of security and the knowledge that he is worthy of unconditional love. Bonding truly begins at birth, and it continues to grow with each passing year. How you bond with your baby, and how soon, will impact his well-being in a way that will last a lifetime.

The Ties That Bind

Stay connected. If you haven't yet delivered, ask your obstetrician or midwife to delay severing the umbilical cord for as long as possible (usually about 15 minutes).

Nurse your baby as soon as possible, ideally within moments after birth. Studies show that infants who experience intense and early bonding benefit from faster weight gain, more successful breast feeding, and higher IQ scores.

Keep the apple in your eye. In the early days, your baby will not be able to focus and will have her eyes closed much of the time. But expressing your love for her through voice and touch will comfort and soothe her.

Keep your eye on the apple. When baby is able to better focus on your face, encourage frequent periods of eye contact. Such sessions help to establish a loving and trustful bond. Always include touch when looking into your baby's eyes; stroke her head, face, or hands.

There's nothing like the feel of a warm, tiny body next to your own. Snuggle with your baby often — while she's sleeping or nursing, or just when you both would enjoy a few moments alone together.

When from the wearying war
of life
I seek release,
I look into my baby's face
And there find peace.

— Martha F. Crow

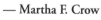

Protect Baby from Sunburn

Young children need extra protection from the sun's rays. When baby's going to be in the sun, be sure to safeguard her delicate skin with either a sunscreen or a sunblock. What's the difference between these products? Sunblocks contain mineral salts such as titanium dioxide that reflect the sun's rays away from tender skin. Sunscreens allow for the absorption of a small amount of UV rays but filters them into harmless infrared wavelengths.

Sun Safety

Use natural products, but know what they contain. The only FDA-approved natural sunscreen component is PABA (para-aminobenzoic acid), a vitamin B derivative. Other agents commonly found in commercial sunscreen products include octyl methoxycinnamate (obtained from cinnamon or cassia), octyl salicylate (derived from sweet birch, wintergreen, and willow), and other botanicals that offer anti-inflammatory or antioxidant qualities, such as aloe vera, black walnut, milk thistle, green tea extract, chamomile, eucalyptus, and mint.

Mommy's Best Sunscreen Oil

Sesame seed oil is a natural sunscreen and nourishing to skin as well. This recipe is formulated for babies, but the whole family will enjoy using it.

> ½ cup cocoa butter
> ¼ cup aloe vera gel
> ¼ cup sesame oil
> ¼ cup sweet almond oil
> contents of 5 vitamin E capsules
> 10 drops lavender essential oil
> 8 drops chamomile essential oil

1. In a saucepan or double boiler set over low heat, combine cocoa butter, aloe vera gel, sesame oil, and sweet almond oil. Heat just until the cocoa butter has melted. Remove from heat.

2. Add vitamin E and essential oils; stir well. Let cool completely.

3. Pour the cooled mixture into two or three small recycled plastic squirt bottles. Shake before each use. Store up to 1 month without refrigeration.

Limit exposure. Babies less than one year old can burn quite easily. And if they're very young, they cannot escape the sun by crawling away or express to you that they've been exposed too long. Never leave a baby sitting on a blanket or in a stroller in direct sunlight for more than 10 minutes.

Make baby fashionable. Give her a snazzy sun hat with a visor to shield her scalp and face. It's even more fun if *you* wear one that matches!

If a burn should occur, combine 2 teaspoons of sweet almond oil and 1 drop of lavender essential oil and gently rub it into baby's skin. Or, apply a small amount of 100 percent pure aloe vera gel to the area.

Here's another soothing burn remedy: Fill baby's bath with equal amounts of warm water and apple cider vinegar. The vinegar helps reduce redness and pain and restores the pH mantle of the skin. Be careful not to let this solution get in baby's eyes!

Nursing Is Good for Both of You

There's no doubt that breast milk is the perfect food for your baby. Nursing fosters a close bond between mother and child and helps reduce your baby's risk of allergies, asthma, and a host of diseases. Nursing offers other benefits for mom, too: It burns calories and helps the uterus return to its normal size.

Tips for Nursing

Whenever possible, choose a quiet, restful place to nurse. The more at ease you are when nursing, the more successful both you and baby will be in your mission.

The earlier you start, the better. Ideally, you should first nurse your newborn within an hour after delivery, when the sucking instinct will be quite strong. At this early stage, your breasts won't be producing milk but rather a fluid called colostrum that contains protective antibodies.

Nurse on demand. And newborns *do* demand to be fed often, about every two hours. Don't worry, you won't run out of milk! In fact, the more often you nurse, the more milk you'll produce.

Engorgement of the breasts is common in the first few days after birth. You'll find relief from — you guessed it — nursing. Or, you can relieve the discomfort with warm baths or compresses. You can also save milk by collecting it with a breast pump and storing it in the refrigerator or freezer. This allows fathers and caregivers to feed the baby as well.

Get into the right position. Believe it or not, a baby's jaw has 3 times the strength of an adult's, so baby will readily latch on when he's hungry. Proper positioning will help reduce soreness for mom and make less work for baby. Make sure you place the nipple as far back in the baby's mouth as possible.

Avoid in-between snacks. Supplementing a nursing baby with formula or sugar water will spoil his appetite for mother's milk.

While breast feeding may be natural, it isn't necessarily a given that everything will go smoothly. Both you and your baby are learning this process; if you don't feel you're both on the same page of the book, your midwife, physician, or local Le Leche League representative can help you. (See Resources for contact information.)

MAKE YOURSELF COMFORTABLE

When you first begin nursing your baby, you will quickly learn that your milk flow seems to magically turn "on" whenever your baby cries from hunger. This is known as the "letdown reflex" and it's a perfectly normal and desirable response. It's interesting to note that this reaction usually occurs only when your own baby cries and not in response to another.

While this built-in mechanism ensures that your baby's needs are met, it can lead to embarrassing moments for you. Plan to wear plenty of old sweatshirts and flannel shirts until you and your baby become more in sync with a feeding schedule. Special pads or even ordinary cotton cloths tucked into a nursing bra can help to absorb any leakage.

23

Guilt-Free Bottle Feeding

There are scores of reasons why a new mother might elect to bottle feed rather than breast feed, every one of them valid. It's ironic that breast feeding (especially in public) was once considered "radical." Today, the tables have turned, and a mother can sometimes feel guilty or inadequate for not participating in this practice. But most doctors agree that bottle feeding is a perfectly adequate substitute for breast feeding.

The important thing to remember is that how you feed your baby is entirely your decision and that you must do what is comfortable for you and your lifestyle. Try not to imagine that you're being given sideways glances of disapproval. Have faith in the old adage that "mother knows best."

Formula for Success

Here are a few things to remember to help you keep an even keel and keep baby happy and comfortable if you choose to bottle feed.

Is the combination route right for you? Many new mothers choose to start out breast feeding and then switch to formula soon after birth. This offers the benefit of giving your baby much-needed antibodies at the start before adapting to the bottle. When it's time, most babies will accept the "other" nipple just as readily as they do your own. If you encounter any transitional problems, consult your doctor or midwife for advice.

Keep in mind that formula-fed babies thrive just as well as breast-fed babies. In fact, you might have been fed from a bottle — and you turned out great!

Nurturing a baby is not centered solely on the breast. If it were, fathers would be left out in the cold! Rest assured that there are many other ways that you'll be nurturing your infant. Nursing offers a natural way to bond and feel close, but so does bottle feeding — along with bathing, playing, and snuggling.

Try to find a reasonably quiet and secluded place when offering your baby a bottle. Too much activity or noise at feeding time can distract baby and possibly contribute to digestive upset if she has to turn her head to find its source.

Never grab a bottle straight from the refrigerator and give it to your baby. Instead, let the formula come to room temperature. You can also warm it slightly in the microwave (loosen the cap first!) for 20–30 seconds. If you do this, always test the temperature of the formula on the inside of your wrist to make sure it isn't too hot for your baby.

24

Table Talk

As soon as your baby is old enough to sit without support, she's ready to join the family at the dinner table for mealtimes, even if eating solid foods is still a spectator sport for her. But when she becomes interested in learning the skill of fine dining, you'll need to muster up all the patience, encouragement, and clean washcloths you can spare. Here are a few ways to make the transition to solids a pleasant one.

Let's Eat!

Safety comes first! Make sure your high chair is certified by the Juvenile Products Manufacturers

Association (JPMA). This should be identified by a seal on the packaging or on the chair itself. If there is any doubt, you can call JPMA at (609) 231-8500. Always make full use of the restraining belts and straps when your baby is in the high chair. Chairs with removable trays make cleanup easier and will allow you to simply pull it up to the table sans tray when baby is older. Never leave your baby unattended in a high chair.

Introduce baby to her first table meals after she's had a mini meal from the breast or bottle. This will encourage her to experiment with new foods, and with a little food in her tummy, she'll be less likely to become anxious or frustrated than if she were very hungry.

Let baby get a grip. Baby's first spoon for self-feeding should be made from PVC-free plastic, since metal can irritate gums and new teeth. A curved handle allows little hands to get a firm grasp and reduces the risk of a poke to the eye, nose, or nearby sibling.

Don't use bibs that tie around the neck; they present a possible choking hazard. Instead, use bibs with snaps or Velcro tabs that you can easily pull free. If you're the creative type (and I know you are), you can make your own bibs from old T-shirts or scrap fabric.

If baby's shirt or top becomes very soiled during a feeding, pull his arms out of the garment and then carefully roll it up to remove it. This will prevent food from adhering to his face or hair.

Expect what you put in to come back out. Babies are messy eaters, but not intentionally. They're used to a liquid diet and at first simply lack the coordination to chew and swallow solid food. Try not to fuss when your baby spits out her food, even if most of her meal lands on the table or floor. However, avoid looking amused when her mashed peas cascade down her chin, or it will become a game. In short, offer simple praises for positive eating habits and try to ignore the negative.

Older siblings often enjoy spoon feeding their younger brother or sister. But, while this may free your hands for a few moments, don't wander off to another part of the house to do something else. You'll need to supervise the feeding anyway to make sure your older child isn't getting too much food in the baby's mouth at once.

Now, as always, the most automated appliance in a household is the mother.

— Beverly Jones

Natural Baby Food Made Easy

Baby's first solid food won't be truly solid — it's more like liquefied versions of adult foodstuffs. Cooked and mashed sweet potatoes, squash, apples, carrots, avocados, bananas, and cereals with liquid added will be the standard fare for beginners. Check with your pediatrician for a list of foods and a schedule that's right for your little one.

Baby Food Basics

Introduce one new food at a time and watch for signs of allergy, such as diarrhea, rashes, or respiratory problems. The general rule is to let five days elapse between introducing different food items.

Whenever possible, select organic fruits and vegetables that are certified to be free of synthetic pesticides and fertilizers. Most supermarkets carry organic foods, but if yours doesn't, you might consider joining a food co-op or growing your own.

Cow's milk is really quite indigestible for humans and is a common source of allergies, especially in the first year. For a healthy alternative, use soy or rice milk when making cereals or mashed foods.

Make baby food in quantity to be canned or frozen for later use. Homemade baby food will stay fresh in the refrigerator for one to two days and in the freezer for two months. You might want to invest in a canning pot, but a large pot to sterilize jars and lids will do.

Good Start Cereal

Simple, nutritious, and purely delicious!

   1 cup rolled oats
   ½ cup soy or rice milk (vanilla flavor is good)
   ½ cup pure apple juice
   ½ banana, mashed

1. Combine all ingredients in a microwave-safe bowl and microwave on high for 2 minutes.

2. For beginning eaters, pour cooked cereal into a blender or food processor and blend with additional soy milk as needed to make a smooth puree.

Quinoa & Sweet Potato Porridge

Quinoa, long considered one of the world's most perfect and versatile foods, is a gluten-free product with a nutty flavor and similar in texture to millet. The addition of sweet potato to this recipe gives the cereal color and sweetness.

>   2 cups water
>   I cup quinoa, rinsed
>   I sweet potato, peeled and cubed

1. Bring the water to a boil. Add the quinoa and sweet potato cubes. Reduce heat and simmer, stirring occasionally, until sweet potato cubes are tender, about 20 minutes.

2. Pour cooked porridge into a blender or food processor and puree. Add a little soy or rice milk to make it smoother.

Spinach & Cheese "Soufflé"

If your child is lactose-intolerant, substitute a combination of ¼ cup of diced tofu and ¼ cup of soy or rice milk (mixed in a blender) or an egg substitute for the cheeses.

>   I pound organic spinach, washed
>   I egg, lightly beaten
>   ½ cup grated parmesan cheese
>   ¼ cup cottage cheese

1. Place the washed spinach, still damp, in a nonstick skillet; heat over very low heat until just wilted, about 1 minute.

2. In a large bowl, combine beaten egg, parmesan cheese, and cottage cheese; mix well. Add wilted spinach to the egg-cheese mixture; mix well.

3. Pour the mixture into a lightly greased casserole and bake until set, 20–30 minutes. Let cool; then puree in a food processor or baby-food grinder to the right consistency for your baby's age.

26

Chase Away Colic

Trapped gas is painful for your baby, and its occurrence can challenge you long into the night, too. A colicky baby appears to be in pain and may cry for long periods. He might draw his legs up in discomfort. Baby might be able to release a few gas blasts on his own, but there are some simple things you can do to help things along.

What a Relief!

A baby might find relief if you place her on her tummy and rub the small of her back in rhythmic, circular motions.

Baby bicycle movements can work wonders to release gas. Gently hold your baby's ankles and slowly move his legs as though pedaling a bike.

If you are nursing, consider whether or not your diet is causing your baby's gas. Beans and certain vegetables, such as broccoli and asparagus, are notorious gas producers.

If you're bottle feeding your baby, make sure the nipple is properly positioned and that the baby is held slightly upright to prevent him from taking in too much air.

Massage baby with the "waterwheel" stroke. With baby lying on her back, gently stroke her stomach with warm, lightly oiled palms. Each hand should glide and pass over the other.

Colic Relief Massage Oil

Dill has long been used to soothe colic and to help babies get to sleep. The aroma of this formula is reminiscent of the old-fashioned "gripe" water sometimes given to colicky babies.

- 1 drop dill essential oil
- 1 tablespoon sweet almond oil

Blend the oils together in a small cup. Spread the oil on your hands and rub your hands together briskly to warm them before massaging your baby.

27

Your Baby Rocks!

Babies just naturally love music. Although you might have exposed baby to many different beats while he was in utero, he most likely will prefer a specific kind of music once he enters the world. Harvard researchers have found that when babies sampled "consonant" or melodic music and then heard the same piece with a "dissonant" arrangement using minor second chords, they showed a distinct preference for the consonant tunes. In other words, the old adage holds true that soothing music calms the savage breast — or, in this case, your wiggling, restless, stimulation-seeking bundle of energy in a diaper. So make music part of the daily life that you share with your child.

The Old Song and Dance

Music does more than entertain; it enhances brain development. A study recently published in *Neurological Research* shows that music training in preschoolers strengthens the spatial and abstract reasoning abilities needed to excel in math and science. Early appreciation of music will boost your budding engineer's chances of success.

Music for babies isn't just about Mary's little lamb anymore! There are excellent CDs and videos available for even the youngest of infants that include classical tones and multicultural themes. There are some that even mimic a baby singing. See Resources for suggestions.

Dance is an extended expression of the love of music. Dance with your baby to whatever music moves you (or her).

Hold a family sing-a-long. No matter how creaky you think you sound, you'll be sure to elicit delightful applause from baby.

Music at bedtime can be just the thing to send baby to dreamland. Don't let her fall completely asleep to the music, though; she might get in the habit of waking up when the music stops.

Cleanliness Is Only Natural

Baby's skin and hair seem so perfect and new — shouldn't you use products with perfectly natural ingredients to wash them? Commercial shampoos and soaps — even those designed for little ones — can contain some pretty harsh agents that will irritate skin. You can purchase vegetable- and botanical-based soaps from a health food store (see Resources for recommendations) or try one of the simple formulas suggested here.

A Clean Baby Is a Happy Baby

Nothing could be simpler than creating your own all-natural baby washes and shampoos. With a few easy-to-find, economical ingredients, you'll be bathing baby in gentle, effective, and fragrant soaps.

Make sure the room where baby is bathed is warm and free of drafts. Take care to avoid getting soapy water into your baby's eyes. When washing or rinsing hair, support your baby's neck and head on your arm so that water runs away from her face. Make sure your baby doesn't handle the soap and then place her fingers near her eyes or mouth.

Herbal Soap Balls

These little balls of soap are great for the whole family to use. To make them last longer, dry out the soap dish after use or remove soap from the shower between uses.

- 3 bars unscented castile soap, grated
- 2 tablespoons sweet almond oil
- 1 ½ tablespoons lanolin
- 3 tablespoons ground oatmeal
- 2 tablespoons dried, crushed lavender (leaves and flowers)
- 6 drops lavender essential oil

1. In a double boiler set over medium heat, heat the grated soap, sweet almond oil, and lanolin until completely melted, stirring occasionally. Remove from heat and stir in remaining ingredients.

2. With oiled hands, scoop up small amounts of the soap mixture and form balls about the size of a lemon. Place the soap balls on waxed paper and let stand until completely cooled and hardened. Use as you would regular soap.

Glycerin Herbal Soap

Glycerin bars are very gentle and moisturizing, and they can be found in almost any supermarket or pharmacy. These soaps will disappear quickly if left in a puddle of water in the soap dish, so keep them dry between uses.

- 3 bars glycerin soap, unscented
- 1 tablespoon sweet almond oil
- 5 drops rose otto essential oil

1. Chop the glycerin soap into chucks with a sharp knife and melt completely in a double boiler set over medium heat. Remove from heat; blend in the oils.

2. Pour the mixture into ungreased soap molds. (These are available in craft stores in fun shapes.) You can also use small, clean plastic containers or lids as molds. If you pop the molds into the freezer, they'll be set in 30–45 minutes. When completely cool, tap out the soaps and wrap in tissue paper until ready to use.

Pure & Simple Shampoo and Body Wash

It doesn't get any easier than this! Pure castile soap is made from coconut or olive oil and is very gentle. Dr. Bronner's is my favorite brand.

- 4 drops chamomile essential oil
- 2 drops lavender essential oil
- 1 bottle (16 ounces) liquid castile soap, unscented

1. Place the essential oils in the container of castile soap. Replace the lid and shake well.

2. To use as a body wash, just squeeze out a teaspoonful onto a moist cotton washcloth. You can also use this formula as a shampoo, but be careful not to let it get into baby's eyes.

Take Care of Those New Teeth

Some babies sprout a tooth or two without any problem at all — much to the surprise of their parents when making the discovery one morning! Other babies seem to get one tooth at a time for an agonizing eternity. But the teething process is usually steady and spans anywhere from the ages of three months to three years.

Protect Those Pearly Whites

Look for the signs. Some signs that your baby is teething include the appearance of red cheeks, a temporary loss of appetite, irritability (you won't miss this one), and increased drooling (although three-month-olds typically drool more often anyway). Contrary to popular belief, teething is never indicated by fever. If fever is present, take it as a sign of illness.

Teething rings can seem like a lifesaving toy for both you and your baby. Get the kind that you can fill with water and freeze. The coolness will ease painful inflammation of the gums while the hardness will help the tooth make its escape to the surface. (*Note:* Make sure the teething ring is PVC-free. See Tip 16 for more information.)

Keep new teeth clean. The time to begin a cleaning regimen begins as soon as the first tooth has emerged. You can clean a sole tooth or a scant few with a damp washcloth or piece of gauze. When several teeth appear, it's time for a baby toothbrush. You should not use commercial toothpaste until your child is at least two (in part due to the fluoride content and because your child will likely swallow it), but after that, non-fluorinated, unsweetened natural toothpastes are available from your health food store. Tom's of Maine is an excellent brand. Check with your dentist or pediatrician.

Avoid dental problems before they start. Never let your baby go to sleep with a bottle, even if it's just water. Bacteria can linger on the nipple, and liquid may find its way to the inner ear, causing ear infections. Always clean baby's teeth after a meal and especially before bedtime.

Give your baby foods to teethe by. A frozen popsicle (all natural and without sweeteners, please) or a frozen banana can work wonders on sore gums. But be sure to remove the item when it begins to thaw; otherwise, small pieces could begin to break off, presenting a choking hazard. Older babies and toddlers might prefer hard toast or biscuits, but again, make sure there's no danger of choking. If the biscuit contains sugar, clean your baby's teeth soon after eating, or at least have her drink some water until you can clean them. Always make sure your baby is sitting upright when teething on foods, and remain nearby to supervise.

A tree is an aerial garden, a botanical migration from the sea, from those earliest plants, the seaweeds; it is a purchase on crumbled rock, on ground. The human, standing, is only a different upsweep and artic- ulation of cells. How treelike we are, how human the tree.

— Gretel Ehrlich

Baby First Aid

Always consult with your health care practitioner when your baby shows signs of illness. An infant's immune, digestive, and respiratory systems are underdeveloped, and it is inappropriate to treat any related disorder yourself. But for those outward bumps, bruises, minor cuts, and rashes, there are a few simple and natural remedies you can use to promote healing. *Note:* These treatments should be used only on children older than three months.

Easy At-Home Remedies

Bruises: Arnica *(Arnica montana)*, commonly known as mountain daisy, is a member of the aster family. Arnica reduces pain and inflammation; it is available in gels and spray form from your natural health food store. Arnica is toxic, however, so never use it on broken skin and keep it out of reach of children and pets.

Diarrhea: Oral antibiotics (like those given to treat ear infections) can cause an upset in healthy intestinal flora, and diarrhea can result. Not only is yogurt a nutritious food for even beginning eaters, it's also loaded with "friendly" bacteria that check harmful bacteria in the intestines. However, make sure the brand that you buy specifies that it contains *live cultures*. Health food stores carry reputable brands that have the added benefit of soy. (*Note:* Severe diarrhea, or diarrhea that lingers for more than two days, should be brought to the attention of a physician right away.)

Burns: Whether they're caused by the sun or another source, burns are painful at any age. To treat a minor burn, blend 1 teaspoon of sweet almond oil with 1 drop of lavender essential oil and smooth over the area. Or, squeeze a bit of juice from the leaf of an aloe vera plant and rub it on the area.

Bee Stings: Make a cold compress by dipping a cloth in a solution of ½ cup of cold water, ½ cup of cider vinegar, and 2 drops of chamomile essential oil. Apply the compress to the affected area for several minutes. If allergic reactions (such as swelling of extremities) to the bee sting appear, seek medical attention immediately.

Scrapes and Cuts: In a double boiler set over low heat, slowly melt 2 tablespoons of beeswax, 1 tablespoon of shea butter, and 1 teaspoon of glycerin (available from pharmacies or craft stores). Remove from heat and stir in the contents of 2 vitamin E capsules and 1 drop each of lavender, chamomile, and yarrow essential oils. Pour the mixture into a jar and let cool completely before using. Apply lightly to affected areas.

We say "I love you" to our children, but it's not enough. Maybe that's why mothers hug and hold and rock and kiss and pat.

— Joan McIntosh

31

Give Baby the World

The natural world is like a fine tapestry crafted from living thread, a place of continual wonderment. Teaching your baby simple ways to appreciate nature will encourage responsible citizenship on this big blue marble of ours. You might even learn, or relearn, a few things!

Natural Wonders

Romance your baby in the moonlight. On a clear night, step outside to observe the glow of the moon and the twinkling of the stars. You might even make a wish together.

Stop and smell the roses. Babies delight in smelling different things. Remember, the sense of smell is the only sense fully developed at birth. Grow an aromatic flower garden and let baby sample all the different aromas it has to offer. Or, tour public gardens or parks with beautiful plantings.

Serve your centerpiece for dinner. Many flowers are quite edible, and they make very unusual and attractive additions to soups, salads, and desserts. If baby is adept at finger foods, let her sample one or two petals in her pudding or yogurt. Some examples of edible flowers are snapdragons, roses, nasturtiums, violets, and lavender blossoms. *Note:* Never give your child any flowers that have been treated with pesticides or other chemicals. If you're not sure if a flower has been grown organically, don't use it. In addition, explain to baby that flowers should only be eaten from the kitchen, not the garden.

Take baby on a picnic. If it's a breezy day, you can both lie on your backs on a blanket and watch the clouds roll by and change shapes.

Head for the beach. The sights, sounds, and textures of the shore will captivate your baby. Let her feel the sand between her fingers, stroke a seashell, and dip her toes in the water. Just remember to protect her delicate skin from the sun! (See page 55.)

32

Keep Baby's Environment Clean and Safe

Ordinary household cleansers are full of chemicals that are harmful to both humans and the environment. Why use them around your baby?

The Naturally Clean Home

Visit your local health food store to learn about organic, nontoxic products for garden, pets, and laundry. Commercial laundry products are toxic, and home and garden pesticides are associated with an increased risk of brain cancer and leukemia in children. Even the most ordinary household products pose a threat if handled or swallowed.

You can make a simple and effective liquid dish-washing soap from liquid castile soap. Notice I don't call it detergent? Detergents often contain a mind-boggling list of synthetic chemicals that help the mixture retain its stability during shipment and exposure to different temperatures and light intensities. Dr. Bronner's castile soap is available with lavender or peppermint essential oils already added for scent and extra cleaning power. Or, you can add a few drops of your favorite essential oils to a bottle that is unscented.

If you have an automatic dishwasher, consider using a natural washing product that is nontoxic and readily biodegradable. My favorite brands are Seventh Generation and Shaklee's Basic D (a concentrate that lasts for months!).

Instead of using wood cleaners and polishes, try simple Murphy's Oil Soap. Most wood doesn't need polishing anyway, just periodic cleaning. If you wish, you can add a few drops of cedar essential oil right to the bottle for that fresh, woodsy scent when dusting.

Replace your kitchen cleaners with an herbal degreaser. Fill a 22-ounce spray bottle with equal amounts of water and vinegar and 20 drops of sweet orange oil.

Clean windows and other glass with a solution of 1 cup vinegar and 1 cup water.

For a natural spray disinfectant, fill a 22-ounce spray bottle with 1½ of cups vinegar, 1 cup of water, and 15 drops *each* of thyme, rosemary, and tea tree essential oils.

Always store your natural cleaners and the ingredients used to make them away from children and pets. Just because they are organic and nontoxic doesn't mean that they cannot still cause illness, allergic reaction, or skin irritation if handled or swallowed.

There are many good books on natural cleaning that are loaded with recipes and ideas, such as my book *The Naturally Clean Home: 101 Safe and Easy Herbal Formulas for Nontoxic Cleansers* (Storey Books, 1999).

Your health food store will usually have several types of organic household products in stock. Many such stores also carry magazines and books with additional information and resources.

Baby's Day Out

Where to go and what to do with baby? Babies love stimulation and learning about the world around them. Here are a few great tips for how to make the most of your afternoons together.

Take a Field Trip

Take a hike. This is a time when the sling (see page 20 for more information) is wonderful to wear in front, so baby can see what you're seeing and not where you've been. To prevent injury to either of you, make sure you hike on a clear path, away from rocky ledges and tree branches.

Pack a picnic lunch and head for the park or playground. Don't forget the pail, the shovel, and some sunscreen!

Go for a swim. Newborns take to water naturally. After all, they spend nine months immersed! Whether it's in your backyard pool or the community pool at the YMCA, your baby will find floating in water very soothing. Skip the water wings, though; they can slip off or tangle on little arms. The Diaper Swim Vest is a new device from 1-2-3 Swim (800-936-6243) that allows even the smallest of babies to safely float on their backs. You can use it in the tub, too! Supervision is required.

Tour a museum. Your baby will find something interesting to look at in any kind of museum, from art to science to natural history. Babies love to look at pictures, so if art is your thing, you can amuse yourself, too — just make sure it's a place you can exit quickly if baby doesn't share your enthusiasm for modern art!

Head for the zoo. What a blast it will be for baby to see all the baby animals! And the day won't be complete unless you mimic the sound each animal makes. Baby will be entertained and educated, too.

Rock-a-Bye Baby

Parenthood is a wonderfully happy time, but it can also be stressful, especially when your baby has difficulty sleeping. Here are some simple ideas to make bedtime a happy occasion for all.

Nighty-Night

Establish a regular routine. Start out with a soothing herbal bath and then perhaps a snuggling or nursing session. Rocking is another calming activity. The last step of the routine, from a favorite story to a poem or lullaby, should always take place in the baby's crib or bed.

Try not to let your baby fall asleep with you on the couch or on your bed at night. (Of course, this doesn't mean that you shouldn't take afternoon naps together now and then.) Letting baby fall asleep in areas other than his own room is habit forming; he'll want to continue to fall asleep in those places.

Massage, in combination with a story or song, is very relaxing. It doesn't have to be anything fancy — a constant circular motion on the back or belly will do. You can also gently stroke the side of your baby's face or massage her hands.

Purchase lullaby tapes to play softly in the background to help baby help herself to sleep. Look for instrumental melodies, a lilting human voice, or even a rhythmic heartbeat. (See Resources for more information.)

Sleep, my child, and peace attend
  thee
All through the night.
Guardian angels God will send
  thee,
All through the night.
Soft the drowsy hours are creeping
Hill and vale in slumber sleeping.
I my loving vigil keeping,
All through the night.

— Traditional lullaby

Finding Good Child Care

Most parents struggle to meet the demands of home, child rearing, and a career. Even if you work from home or make child rearing your main job, sooner or later another caregiver will come into the picture. In fact, nearly 70 percent of parents with young children place them in some kind of daily care situation. Before hiring outside help, arm yourself with a few common-sense guidelines for finding appropriate and responsible care for your child.

Help Wanted

If you are returning to work after having your baby, you'll probably have someone care for your child in your own home. A relative might be the best choice, but a trusted friend or neighbor can become part of your child's extended family as well. You can also ask friends and neighbors for recommendations.

If you're hiring a nanny or au pair, hire one through a reputable agency that can conduct a thorough background check, including a criminal record investigation. According to the International Nanny Association, about 5 percent of nannies applying for a job have criminal convictions. Most of these are attracted to newspaper ads and agencies that will not check their backgrounds.

Thoroughly interview your in-home caregiving candidates at least twice. Why do they want to work with young children? Do they share your attitudes about child rearing? Why did their last job end? Play the "What if" game and ask questions about how they would handle specific situations. Follow through by contacting references.

If you are considering a day-care center for your older baby, talk with other parents whose children have attended or currently attend the center. Discuss the center's policies toward illness, emergency closings, and other important issues so you know what to expect when a situation arises.

A childcare home, where a primary adult provides care in his or her own home, is another option. Interview and spend some time with the adult in charge. Is the home licensed and regularly inspected? How many children will this person be caring for each day? Will your child receive the attention appropriate for her age?

Whether your childcare arrangements are in-home or away from home, exercise your right to an open door policy. Make occasional surprise visits to observe what's going on when you're not present.

Most of all, trust your gut. If any red flags about your care provider surface, or if your child begins to respond negatively to a care provider, you will need to reevaluate the situation and make changes accordingly.

Children are likely to live up to what you believe of them.

— Lady Bird Johnson

Fun with Finger Foods

Babies go through a series of steps in learning to pick up finger foods. At first they use the side of the palm to scoop food pieces toward them. At about six months, babies will begin to draw food pieces to the palm with the fingers but not the thumb. Finally, between six and ten months, babies develop the pincer grasp, in which the thumb and forefinger come together, making the transport of food from hand to mouth more precise.

Baby, Feed Thyself

Just as the transition to solid foods was a milestone for baby, the moment that she begins to feed herself without much help from you is an important step in her development. Baby will be tempted to put just about anything in her mouth at this stage, so it's important that you monitor closely what's going in there.

Always watch your baby while she's eating. Food items or pieces should be small enough that they won't become lodged in the throat if swallowed. Before the age of three, don't give baby items such as nuts, raisins, pieces of hard fruit, raw vegetable sticks, and nut butters, which pose a choking hazard.

Tofu Fingers

These little treats pack a punch of protein and savory flavor. Watch them disappear!

- I package firm tofu, drained
- I ½ tablespoons tamari
- ¼ cup wheat germ
- I tablespoon sesame seeds
- ½ cup plain breadcrumbs

1. Preheat oven to 350°F.

2. Slice tofu into small strips; using a basting brush, lightly coat tofu pieces with tamari.

3. In a blender or food processor, grind the wheat germ and sesame seeds for 1 minute. On a plate, combine the ground wheat germ and sesame seed mixture with the breadcrumbs.

4. Roll the tofu fingers in the crumb mixture and place on a lightly oiled baking sheet. Bake for 15–20 minutes, until golden brown.

What can you let your baby feed himself? Give him small pieces of soft fruits, such as banana, mango, peaches, watermelon (without seeds), pears, and cantaloupe. Cook vegetables and cut them into cubes; crumble hard-boiled eggs into small pieces; and toast whole grain breads and cut them into small pieces. Small cooked pasta shapes are another good choice. Always give baby just a few bits of food at a time, or he may put too much in his mouth at once.

Mighty Muffins

These tasty muffins are moist and rich in important nutrients and fiber. Makes 12 large muffins or 24 minis.

- 1 ½ cups unbleached flour
- 4 teaspoons baking powder
- 2 teaspoons ground cinnamon
- 1 teaspoon ground ginger
- ½ cup rolled oats
- 2 eggs
- 1 cup natural applesauce
- 1 cup cooked, mashed pumpkin or other squash
- ¼ cup vegetable oil

1. Preheat oven to 400°F.

2. In a large bowl, sift together flour, baking powder, cinnamon, and ginger. Add oats and mix well. Add the eggs, applesauce, pumpkin, and oil; blend batter until smooth.

3. Spoon batter into lightly greased standard or mini muffin tins, filling each three-quarters full. Bake until lightly golden — 20–25 for standard muffins, 15–20 minutes for mini muffins.

Banana Boats

I banana
½ teaspoon brown sugar
½ teaspoon cinnamon
½ teaspoon nutmeg

1. Peel the banana and slice it in half lengthwise.

2. In a small bowl, combine brown sugar, cinnamon, and nutmeg. Sprinkle liberally over banana halves.

3. Broil the banana halves until just warmed, about 1 minute. Cut into small pieces, making sure they are not too warm to handle, and serve.

Fresh Fruit Custard

I cup applesauce
I mashed banana
I cup soy or rice milk
4 eggs, beaten (or the equivalent amount of egg substitute)
I teaspoon vanilla
I teaspoon cinnamon

1. Preheat oven to 350°F. Combine all ingredients and mix well in a blender or food processor.

2. Pour mixture into custard cups or ramekins and sprinkle with additional cinnamon if you wish. Set cups into a shallow pan and add hot water to cover 1 inch of the cup bottoms.

3. Bake for 45–55 minutes, or until a toothpick inserted into the center comes out clean.

4. Chill for at least 1 hour and serve. (*Note:* The custard will keep in the refrigerator for up to 3 days.)

Games Babies Play

Playtime is learning time for your baby, and until he's two or three, you are his primary and favorite playmate. Here are a few ways you both can get the most from playtime.

Fun & Games

Babies up to six months love the "I'm gonna getcha" game. From a short distance, slowly "stalk" baby while chanting "I'm gonna getcha!" At first, baby may look puzzled, even alarmed, but he'll soon get the pattern and realize that he can trust you. It's even better if the final "getcha" is accompanied with a raspberry to the neck.

Don't go overboard and overstimulate your baby. She'll let you know when she's had enough by crying or simply looking away from you. Take these gestures as a signal that it's time to cuddle instead.

The classic peek-a-boo game delights most babies. While they don't fully comprehend that they haven't actually disappeared, they find the idea that you don't know where they are a laugh riot! Toss a light blanket or towel over baby's head, wait a moment, and then say, "Where's baby?" a few times. Then lift a corner and say, "There you are! Peek-a-boo!" Soon after learning this game, baby will forego the head covering and will dash away to hide as soon as you say "Where's baby?"

Childproof your baby's play areas as much as possible to allow him freedom for walking, cruising, or crawling. Store toys in cartons on a low shelf or on the floor to make access for baby (and cleanup for you) easier.

Give baby a problem. Give your six- to nine-month-old an object to hold in each hand; then offer her a third object to hold. With repetition, your baby will eventually learn to solve the dilemma by releasing one object to pick up another.

Put action behind the words. Babies eight months old or older love songs accompanied by finger and hand movements that help tell the story. You can probably recall such song-games as Pat-a-Cake and Itsy-Bitsy Spider from your childhood.

LITTLE PIGGIES

Babies love rhymes that involve the tickling of body parts, especially toes. Here's a classic that begins with the big toe and ends with the smallest:

This little piggy went to market, this little piggy stayed home.

This little piggy had roast beef, this little piggy had none.

And this little piggy cried, "Wee, wee, wee," all the way home.

(*Note:* Substitute "tofu" for "roast beef" if your baby is a vegetarian.)

Being a mother enables one to influence the future.

— Jane Sellman

Born to Learn

Babies are like sponges; they are willing to absorb everything. In fact, half of an infant's brain growth occurs in the first six months of life, up to 85 percent in the first year. The first year of learning affects not only their mental development but their personality traits as well. It's not advisable to try to mold your baby into a neurosurgeon or Nobel prize winner with slide shows and documentaries, but there are simple things you can do each day to improve his quality of mental stimulation. Spending time with your baby in this way will also help to develop a strong bond between the two of you that will last long after his childhood toys and trinkets are put away.

Be Her First Teacher

Engage your baby in activities that involve all the senses as much as possible. Smell things. Encourage laughter and song. Compare the textures of different everyday objects.

Action videos geared for baby can help her to identify objects and other people and to follow sequential events. Watch along with her and talk about what you see.

Babies 12 months and older are beginning to view the world beyond their own existence. Encourage a broad world-view with books, music, videos, and events that embrace cultural and racial diversity. Teaching tolerance and acceptance now will have a lasting impact.

Babies age 6 to 12 months adore imitating sounds and facial expressions. Make a game of making the appropriate sound when looking at animal pictures. Let her see your facial expressions often; this is one of the earliest forms of communication she'll use.

Nurture your baby's brain. Select toys and activities that will promote active learning, exploration, age-appropriate problem solving, and a sense of accomplishment. Toys such as discovery books or playmats entertain a baby while she learns about the world by "discovering" their hidden secrets. These items may include appealing things such as a ladybug resting under a leaf-shaped flap of felt, bold images of animals against a high-contrast pattern, or different textures to experience. Take your time discovering these objects with your baby. You can help her to identify specific objects by name or even make up stories about them.

Seize opportunities. Point out different colors and shapes or recite the ABCs while you and your baby are sitting in traffic or waiting for a doctor's appointment.

BABY'S COLORS

What's black, white, and red all over? A newborn can see your face from a distance of about 6 inches, but until six to eight weeks of age, he cannot distinguish its features. And, while adults may find the traditional pastel colors of "pretty in pink" and "baby-boy blue" appealing, your baby cannot see in full color until he's about four months old.

Black, white, and red toys display pictures and objects against a high-contrast background on rattles, playmats, blankets, mobiles, and activity centers. They are designed to challenge infants under the age of four months.

39

Baby Skin Lotions and Potions

Babies have such soft, sweet-smelling skin — they deserve equally tender, mild skin care. With simple, readily available ingredients, you can make these skin-nurturing formulas to use after baby's bath, while diapering, or during a massage. The whole family will want to use them! They make great gifts for other babies and parents, too.

Pampering Baby's Skin

With a few simple ingredients from your local herb or health food store, you'll be able to make your own all-natural skin formulas. These formulas are very mild, but it's always wise to perform a patch test before using a new product on your baby's skin. Apply a small amount of the product to baby's inner arm, just above the elbow. Wait 24 hours; if any itching, redness, or other signs of irritation occur, discontinue use immediately.

Beautiful Baby Balm

Use this balm during diaper changes to protect baby's skin.

½ ounce cocoa butter
½ ounce beeswax
1 tablespoon jojoba oil
1 tablespoon glycerin
1 tablespoon rosewater (available in pharmacies)
4 drops chamomile essential oil
4 drops mandarin essential oil

1. In a double boiler set over medium heat, combine cocoa butter, beeswax, and jojoba oil; heat until completely melted. Add glycerin and rosewater; stir.

2. Remove from heat and add essential oils. Scoop into a clean jar and label. Store at room temperature, away from heat and drafts. Discard any unused portion after 6 weeks.

Natural Baby Oil

Use this oil on baby's damp skin after a bath.

6 drops calendula essential oil
2 drops lavender essential oil
2 drops rose otto essential oil
1 bottle (4 ounces) sweet almond oil

Add the essential oils directly to the bottle of sweet almond oil. Shake well before using. This formula will keep its effectiveness for up to 1 year. A bottle this size should last for about 6 months with normal use.

Skin So Silky

This formula is very nourishing for skin and suitable for use by every member of the family.

  1 cup sweet almond oil
  ½ cup cocoa butter
  2 teaspoons lanolin
  ½ ounce beeswax
  ⅔ cup rosewater
  ½ cup aloe vera gel
  6 drops rose otto essential oil
  contents of 2 vitamin E capsules

1. In a double boiler set over medium heat, combine the sweet almond oil, cocoa butter, lanolin, and beeswax; heat until completely melted. Remove from heat and add remaining ingredients.

2. Mix with an electric mixer until smooth and creamy. Scoop into a clean jar and label. Store away from heat. Discard any unused portion after 6 weeks.

WHY USE NATURAL PRODUCTS?

Learn about the properties of ingredients found in many commercial skin care products.

- Lauramide DEA — Used as a thickening agent, it's associated with skin disorders and allergic reactions.
- Sodium laurel sulfate and sodium laureth sulfate — Found in many lotions, these chemicals are highly irritating.
- Propylene glycol — Common skin allergen.
- Mineral oil and petroleum products — Clog pores and deprive cells of oxygen.

Build
Self-Esteem

Nothing influences your child's opinion of himself as much as your opinion of him. Giving your child a positive view of himself right from the start will reap many rewards in the years to come.

"I Like Being Me!"

Your approval shines like a beacon in your tone of voice, your words, your facial expressions, and your body language — and your disapproval is just as obvious. If something your baby has done displeases you, make sure that you target the behavior, not the child.

We'd love your thoughts . . .

Your reactions, criticisms, things you did or didn't like about this Storey Book. Please use space below (or write a letter if you'd prefer — even send photos!) telling how you've made use of the information . . . how you've put it to work . . . the more details the better!

Thanks in advance for your help in building our library of good Storey Books.

Pamela B. Art

Publisher, Storey Books

Book Title: _____

Purchased From: _____

Comments: _____

_____

_____

_____

_____

_____

Your Name: _____

Mailing Address: _____

E-mail Address: _____

☐ Please check here if you'd like our latest Storey's Books for Country Living Catalog, (or call 800-441-5700 to order).

☐ You have my permission to quote from my comments and use these quotations in ads, brochures, mail, and other promotions used to market Storey Books.

Signed _____ Date _____

e-mail=thoughts@storey.com   www.storeybooks.com   PRINTED IN THE USA   11/99

From: _____

BUSINESS REPLY MAIL

FIRST-CLASS MAIL   PERMIT NO. 2   POWNAL VT

POSTAGE WILL BE PAID BY ADDRESSEE

STOREY'S BOOKS FOR COUNTRY LIVING
STOREY COMMUNICATIONS INC
RR1 BOX 105
POWNAL VT 05261-9988

Help your baby to help himself. Before you know it, he will be busy learning how spoons, buttons, and doorknobs work. Help him when he truly needs your help, but let him practice and perfect such skills on his own. As a parent, one of your tasks is to teach self-reliance.

Set a good example. How do you react when you're angry or frustrated? Is this how you want your baby to behave? Ask yourself if you need to work on some of your own behaviors in order to be a good role model.

Show your baby that she is important to you. Set aside time each day to give her your undivided attention.

Catch your baby in the act of being good. Compliment him when he pets the cat in a nice way or when he shares his toys with others. If you get into this habit while your child is very young, one day you'll be able to say, "Thanks for taking out the garbage without being asked."

Show baby your respect. Say "please" and "thank you" to her as often as you do to adults.

Baby Gymnastics

In the first few months of life, babies are learning to control the movements of their arms and legs. You can help those little muscles along with a few simple (and fun!) strengthening exercises.

Let's Get Physical

While baby lies on his back, gently hold his arms at his sides. Alternate raising one over his head and then the other. While you're at it, you can teach the Newtonian principle of what goes up must come down by chanting "Up we go, down we go" with each movement.

Try baby's version of the "medicine ball." Place baby on her stomach on a beach ball and carefully rock her back and forth while supporting her with one hand. Not only is this fun for baby, but it might help to dislodge a gas bubble or two.

Encourage baby to reach out. When she is able to grasp and let go of an object, hold an enticing toy just within her reach. It helps if the toy is a noise-maker or is brightly colored to get her attention.

Do the baby bicycle. Gently grasp your baby's feet and move them in bicycle fashion as though she is pedaling. It won't take long before baby is able to do this exercise on her own.

When your baby is at least three months old and can support his own head, he can do "sit-ups." While holding baby's hands, gently pull him to a sitting position and then lower him back to the floor.

You can create a baby "Stairmaster" by allowing your 9- to 12-month-old to crawl up your staircase (with close supervision) or over a stack of pillows.

Reading Is Rewarding

Reading is certainly an enjoyable activity for both you and your baby, but there are other far-reaching benefits to be gained from it. A recent study conducted at Johns Hopkins University found that babies as young as eight months can recognize and recall words in selected stories repeatedly read to them. Reading to your baby is one way to promote the process of learning language, helping her to develop a vocabulary reserve for her speaking debut later on.

Read All about It

There is an enormous selection of books available for parents to read to their babies. Get a membership card at your local bookstore or visit Web-based bookstores.

Get familiar with your local library. Many libraries host story hours for different age groups and hold meetings and book signings with guest authors. Most libraries also have an interlibrary loan system that allows you to borrow from other libraries materials that yours does not carry. And, for a gift that truly keeps giving, you can get a library card in your child's name.

Get animated when you read to your baby. Babies absorb word patterns, and they'll remember words and phrases that you get excited about. They'll also learn to interpret meanings from the way you raise or lower your voice.

Give your baby a head start. There are programs available that can help you teach your baby to learn to read before reaching school age. (See Resources for more information.)

Build your baby a library. Once your child develops a love of reading — and before that, being read to — you'll feel like you never have enough books on hand. Let family and friends know that books are always on baby's (and your) wish list for gift-giving holidays.

Recommended Reading
for Infants

These titles are great for babies' first year and many are available in "drool-proof" editions in case they make their way to baby's mouth.

- *Goodnight Moon* by Margaret Wise Brown
- *Where the Wild Things Are* by Maurice Sendak
- *Mad about Madeline* by Ludwig Bemelmans
- *Curious George's ABCs* by H.A. Rey and Margaret Rey
- *Clifford, the Big Red Dog* by Norman Bridwell
- *Runaway Bunny* by Margaret Wise Brown
- *White on Black* by Tana Hoban
- *Jamberry* by Bruce Degen
- *Brown Bear, Brown Bear, What Do You See?* by Eric Carle
- *The Snowy Day* by Ezra Jack Keats

Judicious mothers will always keep in mind that they are the first book read, and the last put aside, in every child's library.

— C. Lenox Remond

Different Strokes for Little Folks

Massage is relaxing and comforting for both parent and baby. It offers health-giving benefits by improving circulation, helping digestion, and providing a sense of well-being. Touch is also an excellent way to bond with your little one.

Massage Techniques for Baby

Remove any jewelry before giving a massage to reduce the risk of injury or irritation.

Make sure the room in which you're giving the massage is warm and free of drafts.

Always put the massage oil on your hands first and then rub them together a few times to warm the oil. The perfect oil to use is plain sweet almond oil.

Remove baby's clothing — but you might want to keep the diaper in place, especially if your lovely baby is a boy. Otherwise, you might be in for an unpleasant surprise.

Always ask permission to massage before you begin, even if baby is too young to understand your request or to offer a response. This will help to instill a sense of body ownership and healthy touch when your child is older.

To massage the head and face, use small circular motions with your fingertips around the forehead, brow line, temples, and jaw line. Try to maintain a hand-over-hand action so that one hand is always in motion during the massage. Do not massage near the eyes or the fontanelle (soft spot on top of the head).

If your baby fusses during a massage, take that as her cue that the massage session is over for now. She may be cold, hungry, or just not in the mood at this time.

When massaging arms and legs, simple downward strokes are effective. Don't forget about the fingers and feet!

Babies love having their chest and back rubbed. But avoid doing so when baby has a full tummy or is hungry.

There are several good books available on infant massage. See Resources for some suggestions.

You are the bows from which your children as living arrows are sent forth. The archer sees the mark upon the path of the infinite, and He bends you with his might that His arrows may go swift and far. Let your bending in the archer's hand be for gladness; For even as He loves the arrow that flies, so He loves also the bow that is stable.

— Kahlil Gibran

44

Organize a Play Group

Between 12 and 18 months of age, your baby will begin to enjoy the company of other children. Here are a few suggestions for getting babies together.

Making Friends

Keep them busy. Some good activities for small groups of babies are an entertaining video, a sing-along, or playing with a large assortment of oversized blocks and rattles. If you're feeling very adventurous, you could spread out a plastic tablecloth on the floor and let them create sculptures with homemade play clay (see recipe on page 45).

Babies bring people together! You can meet other parents with babies through friends, neighbors, church, or work, or at the local park or library.

Don't expect play sessions to last long. Children of this age may tolerate playing with others only for brief spans, but this can provide much needed respite for parents. Plan on being together for about one to two hours, once or twice a week.

Keep the number in your group proportionate to the number of adults available to supervise — one adult monitoring no more than three babies is desirable.

Take turns hosting the group. That way all of the parents will have a chance to have a quiet lunch out or run a few errands without a baby in tow.

Older siblings often love getting involved in playing with babies. They add another pair of eyes for supervision, and including them gives them a sense of worthy participation as well.

Remove tables and lamps or other objects from the play area that could be pulled down by an exploring baby or could result in a bump on the head.

45

Special Needs Babies and Parents

If your baby is developmentally or physically challenged, there's a lot you can do to help him (and you) thrive. Talk to your pediatrician about healthy activities for your baby, and try some of the following suggestions.

Special Considerations

Be aware of how your baby responds to stimuli. How does he react to touch, smell, sounds, and visual stimulation? Does one sense get more focus or require more attention than another? Your observations will help you devise activities that assist sensory integration.

Sometimes it's just as important to reduce certain stimuli. For instance, if your baby is working intensely on gross motor skills and finds noise distracting or even frightening, try to eliminate excess noise while she is engaging in growth activities.

Massage is stimulating and has the added effect of balancing emotions for both parent and child. It promotes trust and bonding between the two of you and is an especially beneficial tool if your baby is visually or hearing impaired.

Some babies are "tactile defensive," meaning that they are hypersensitive to touch, especially around the face, neck, and shoulders. You might have to use firmer massage strokes if this is the case. If your baby receives physical therapy, ask the therapist to recommend specific massage strokes.

People are like snowflakes: No two are alike. This applies to your special needs child, too. Resist the temptation of comparing your child to any other, whether challenged or not. Diversity is a blessing.

One of the best things you can do to help your special needs child is to help yourself. Ask for assistance from community services and parental support groups. (See Resources for more information.)

46

Talk Back
(to Yourself)

Confidence makes better parents — and better babies. But sometimes, especially for first-time parents, it can be daunting to imagine being completely responsible for such a fragile bundle of joy. Whenever those thoughts of "Can I really do this?" begin to surface, close your eyes and say one of these affirmations to yourself . . . or say them out loud for the world to hear! In fact, it wouldn't hurt to make the recitation of self-validating affirmations part of a daily ritual. It won't be long before automatic negative thoughts become positive ones and you discover that your inner voice has better things to say about you.

Positive Affirmations for Parents

I am my baby's teacher. But most of what I need to know I will learn from my baby.

My instincts are worth trusting.

I can choose to take or not take advice when it's offered.

Every moment isn't perfect, but I'll miss the ones that matter if I stay "in my head," thinking about what I "should" have done the last time.

I am a capable and loving parent. My thoughts, words, and actions reflect this every day.

There are many challenges ahead, but I am ready to face them with confidence, ability, and humor.

The Language of Baby-Speak

Sometime between four and six months of age, your baby will begin to make deliberate sounds. You might interpret these sounds as merely an exercise of the vocal chords resulting in gibberish, but they are not without meaning. Your baby has been listening to your speech, picking up on subtle variations of tone and pitch, and these early sounds are actually his first attempts at communication. There's so much more to learn!

Can We Talk?

Talk to your baby. Listen to his babble and respond in kind, mimicking his sounds. This assures him that you're paying attention when he speaks to you.

Build baby's vocabulary. Remember, babies "record" many words from stories and songs and warehouse them for use when they're ready for speech. Point out everyday objects, such as a bottle or teddy bear, and name them for baby.

Call things what they are. Use simple words, but use the correct words for objects. For instance, teach her that a cow is a cow, not a "moo-moo."

Songs are a great way to teach the parts of the body. With traditional rhymes such as "This is the way we wash our face," you can reinforce the connection between the label and the body part.

There is a growing trend toward teaching signs to babies to enable them to communicate better. To some degree, we do this automatically. But there is a standard system of simple signs in use that expands a baby's ability to express her ideas and needs. If this idea appeals to you, get a copy of *Baby Signs* by Linda Acredolo, Ph.D., and Susan Goodwyn, Ph.D. (Contemporary Books). This book is loaded with examples and an illustrated chart of more than fifty signs. Be aware that these signs are not the same as standard sign language.

Today's Memories Tomorrow

Before you know it, your crawling, squawking, energy-driven baby will be all grown up. Even though all the milestones seemed to happen "just yesterday," you'll want to preserve such precious moments. Here are a few easy tips that will help you share your memories with your child years from now.

The Way We Were

Keep a scrapbook. Unlike a photo album, scrapbooks contain "scraps" of past events and occasions. Include such items as a snip of hair from baby's first hair cut, a piece of fabric from his favorite teddy, and all the little trinkets he held so dear from his childhood.

Keep a memories box. You'll want to fill it with items such as the birth announcement, the bill for your hospital or birthing room (you'll both get a real kick out of this later, believe me), baby booties, favorite toys, and early works of art. Later, you can add schoolwork and awards organized by grade level.

Photograph, photograph, photograph. Then get your film developed!

Make home videos. If you don't have a camcorder, you can easily rent or borrow one for special occasions. While you'll want to capture such events as baby's first birthday or holiday, don't forget real-life events like bathtime, snuggling with her older brother, or moments when she's a sleeping angel.

Order a time capsule kit from a company such as An Added Touch Gifts. The kit allows family members to write "letters to the future" and includes a book in which to record what life was like way back when. (See Resources for more information.)

Life with Baby, Siblings, and Pets

Imagine how you would feel if your spouse brought home another companion to live with you both, without even consulting you first. Well, that's probably how a toddler or a beloved pet feels when you bring a new baby into the house. Here are a few tips on nurturing a happy and healthy relationship between baby and all of her family ties.

A Time for Everyone

Ideally, dogs and cats should already have plenty of people experience before they're introduced to a new baby.

What does a baby demand most from you? Your time. And that's exactly what siblings and pets are going to miss getting. Carve out some time each day to spend with your other children and play with your pets to remind them that they're special.

The best way to introduce your pet to a new baby is to start before your baby is born. Let pets inspect the baby's room. The more you try to keep them away, the more they'll want to check out the baby after he arrives. They may even perceive the "shoo" treatment as a sign that the baby is a threat.

Show baby how to properly pet your pet. Nobody likes to have his ears and tail pulled! Also teach your baby that fingers, hands, and articles of clothing are not playthings for your pet.

Always supervise your pet and baby when they're together, but do let them interact. With proper handling, your pet will become a longtime, cherished companion for your baby.

Get older siblings in on the act. Let them help you with caring for and playing with your new baby. But be extra alert: A toddler has no idea how much stronger he is than his baby sister, and cannot "put on the brakes" and may lash out if unsupervised.

Get Ready for the Future — Now

It may seem like a long way off right now, but your child's teen years will be here in a blink. Will she go to college? Will she start her own business? The answers to those questions will work themselves out over the years to come, but there are a few things that you can do right now that will help answer the "how will she do it?" part.

It's Never Too Early

Start a custodial savings account for your baby. You'll be surprised at how much small, regular contributions can add up over the long haul. If you put just $10 into this fund each week, your child will have over $9,000 when she is 18 years of age. If you deposit $25 into her account each week, she'll have more than $23,000 — a good start toward college tuition or a business venture.

Another great way to invest in your baby's future is to purchase U.S. series E bonds. Their minimal purchase cost will be returned several times over when the bonds reach maturity.

Did you know that you can prepay for college? In effect, that's what you're doing when you purchase a CollegeSure CD from the College Savings Bank. The interest rate paid on these CDs is proportionate to the rising cost of college tuition, so full coverage is guaranteed. For more information on the College Savings Bank, see Resources.

Be sure your life, disability, and mortgage (if applicable) insurance policies are up-to-date. After all, you'd want your baby to be provided for if something happened to you. If you don't have any kind of insurance, what are you waiting for?

It will be gone before you know it. The fingerprints on the wall appear higher and higher. Then suddenly they disappear.

— Dorothy Evslin

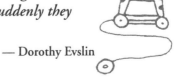

Resources

Childbirth Education, Support & Referrals

Association of Labor Assistants & Childbirth Educators
P.O. Box 382724
Cambridge, MA 02238
(888) 22-ALACE
E-mail: alacehq@aol.com

Doulas of North America
13513 North Grove Dr.
Alpine, UT 84004
(801) 756-7331
Web site: www.dona.org

Birth Resource Network
P.O. Box 881955
San Diego, CA 92188-1955
(619) 525-7753

Adoptive Families of America
(651) 645-9955;
(800) 372-3300
Web site: www.adoptivefam.org

Breastfeeding

Lamaze International
1200 19th St., NW
Suite 300
Washington, D.C. 20036-2422
(800) 368-4404
E-mail: lamaze@dc.sba.com
Web site: www.lamaze-child-birth.com

Breastfeeding National Network
P.O. Box 660
McHenry, IL 60051-0660
(800) TELL-YOU

Organizations for Children with Special Needs

National Parent to Parent Support & Information Systems, Inc. (NPPSIS)
P.O. Box 907
Blue Ridge, GA 30513
(800) 651-1151; (706) 374-3822
Fax: (706) 374-3826
E-mail: NPPSIS@ellijay.com
Web site: www.NPPSIS.org

National Information Clearinghouse for Infants with Disabilities and Life Threatening Conditions (NIC)
(800) 922-9234, ext 201
Information on advocacy, early intervention, parent support, and financial assistance.

MUMS National Parent-to-Parent Network
150 Custer Court
Green Bay, WI 54301-1243
(877) 336-5333
Fax: (920) 339-0995
Matches families with special needs children in 25 countries.

Diapers

The All Together Diaper Company
7362 South Eloni Circle
West Jordan, UT 84084
(801) 566-7579; (877) 215-9004
Web site: www.clothdiaper.com

Earthbaby
300 Lenora St., Suite B-147
Seattle, WA 98121
(877) 375-3600
Web site: www.earthbaby.com

Baby's Wish
P.O. Box 578
Wayne, PA 19087-0578
(888) BABY-WISH;
(888) 222-9947
Web site: www.babyswish.com

Tushies
P.O. Box 5200
West Port, CT 06881
(800) 344-6379
www.tushies.com
Disposable but gel-free diapers.

Slings

The Original Baby Sling (NoJo)
22942 Arroyo Vista
Rancho Santa Margarita, CA
  92688
(800) 440-NOJO
E-mail: info@NoJo.com
www.nojo.com

New Native Baby Carrier
P.O. Box 247
Davenport, CA 95017
(800) 646-1682

Organic Clothing & Bedding

A Happy Planet
PMB #71
2261 Market St.
San Francisco, CA 94114
(888) 946-4277
Web site: www.ahappy
  planet.com

Earthlings
P.O. Box 659
Ojai, CA 93024
(888) GO-BABY-O
E-mail: orders@earthlings.net
Web site: www.earthlings.net

Green Babies
(800) 603-7508
E-mail: mail@greenbabies.com
Web site: www.greenbabies.com

Organic Cotton Alternatives
3120 Central SE
Albuquerque, NM 87106
(888) 645-4452
Web site:
  www.organiccottonalts.com
Futons and bassinets.

White Lotus Futon
191 Hamilton St.
New Brunswick, NJ 08901
(877) HAND MADE
Web site: www.whitelotus.net

Advocates of PVC-Free Plastic & Toys

Greenpeace
1436 U St., NW
Washington, D.C. 20009
(800) 326-0959
Web site: www.greenpeace.org

Children's Health Environ-mental Coalition Network
P.O. Box 846
Malibu, CA 90265
(310) 589-2233
Web site: www.checnet.org

Natural Paints, Finishes & Stains

NonToxiCA, Inc.
1042 Main St., Suite 200
Dunedin, FL 34698
(813) 731-5007
Web site: www.nontoxica.com

Livos Naturals
Livos Phytochemistry
P.O. Box 1740
Mashpee, MA 02649
(518) 477-7955
Web site: www.safepaint.com

Eco Design Co./Natural Choice
1365 Rufina Circle
Santa Fe, NM 87505
(800) 621-2591
Web site:
    www.bioshieldpaint.com

Old Fashioned Milk Paint Co.
436 Main St., P.O. Box 222
Groton, MA 01450-0222
(978) 448-6336
Web site: www.milkpaint.com

Planetary Solutions
2030 17th Street
Boulder, CO 80302
(303) 442-6228
E-mail: paula@planetearth.com

*Natural Vitamins
and Medicines*
Herbs for Kids
1722 14th St. Suite 230
Boulder, CO 80302
(406) 587-0180
Web site: www.herbsfor
    kids.com

Flora, Inc.
P.O. Box 73
805 E. Badger Rd.
Lynden, WA 98264
(800) 446-2110
Web site: www.florainc.com

Organic Foods
Earthbound Farm
1721 San Juan Highway
San Juan Bautista, CA 95045
(888) EAT-ORGANIC
Web site: www.ebfarm.com

Well Fed Baby
(888) WELLFED
Web site: www.wellfedbaby.com

Earth's Best Baby Food
(800) 442-4221
Web site:
    www.earthsbest.com/main.html
Available in natural food stores.

*Natural Baby Soaps
& Lotions*
Earth Friendly Baby
P.O. Box 400
Charlotte, VT 05445
(802) 425-4300
Web site:
    www.earthfriendlybaby.com

Erbaviva
(877) 372-2848
Web site: www.erbaviva.com

Magick Botanicals
3412 West MacArthur Blvd.
Suite K
Santa Ana, CA 92704
(800) 237-0674
Web site:
    www.magickbotanicals.com

Trusted Care
184 West Main St., P.O. Box 690
Tarrytown, NY 10591
(800) 458-2811
Web site: www.trustedcare.com

Weleda, Inc.
P.O. Box 249
175 North Route 9W
Congers, NY 10920
(800) 241-1030
Web site: usa.weleda.com

Publications
Mothering Magazine
P.O. Box 1690
Santa Fe, NM 87504
(800) 984-8116
Web site: www.mothering.com

Nurturing Magazine
#373, 918 - 16th Avenue N.W.
Calgary, Alberta, Canada
  T2M OK3
E-mail: nurturing@nurturing.ca
Web site: nurturing.ca/
  home.htm

Vegetarian Baby and Toddler
P.O. Box 519
Tuolumne, CA 95379-0519
E-mail:
  editor@vegetarianbaby.com
Web site:
  www.vegetarianbaby.com

Working Mother Magazine
135 West 50th St.
New York, NY 10020
(800) 374-3187
Web site:
www.workingmother.com

Natural Toys

Earthwise Basics
214 Elliot St. Suite 2
Brattleboro, VT 05301
(802) 254-4254
Web site: www.naturaltoys.com

First Toys
21 Wrights Crossing Rd.
Pomfret Center, CT 06259
(800) 210-7318
Web site: www.firsttoys.com

Twinkle Toes
(888) 4-TWINKL
Web site: www.twinkletoes.com

Music & Videos

The Baby Store
163 Freelon St.
San Francisco, CA 94107
(877) 551-BABY
E-mail: store@babycenter.com
Web site: store.babycenter.com

Genius Babies
2810 Golf Ridge Dr.
Charlotte, NC 28210
(888) 388-1003
E-mail:
  mailbox@geniusbabies.com
Web site: www.geniusbabies.
  com/genius-babies/music-
  cds2.html

Hap-Pal Music, Inc.
19424 Mayall St.
Northridge, CA 91324
(818) 885-0200
E-mail: hap@netwood.net
Web site: www.happalmer.com

The Infant Learning Company
P.O. Box 189
Bonsall, CA 92003
(888) 732-3888
Web site:
  www.infantlearning.com

Miscellaneous

An Added Touch Gifts
P.O. Box 1836
Waldorf, MD 20604
(301) 638-7778
E-mail:
  info@anaddedtouch.com
Web site:
  www.anaddedtouch.com
*Time capsule kits and other
keepsake gifts.*

College Savings Bank
5 Vaughn Dr.
Princeton, NJ 08540
(800) 888-2723
Web site: www.collegesavings-
  bank.com
CollegeSure CDs.

Index

Nursing
  vs. bottle feeding, 61–63
  and colic, 71
  preparing for, 11, 26
  techniques, 58–60
  when to start, 54
Nutrition, prenatal, 13

O

Oil treatments, 2
  aromatherapy, 8, 9, 25–27
  bathing baby, 37
  colic relief, 71
  cradle cap, 34
  diaper rash, 39–40
  facial, 9
  massage, 11, 15, 116
  and sun, 56, 57

P

Paint, nursery, 22–23, 24
Parenting
  advice, handling 28–30, 123
  affirmations, 122–123
  of newborns, 28–30
Pets, 128–130
Physically challenged babies, 120–121
Pincer grasp, 95
Plastic, in toys, 41–43
Play. See Activities
Powder, baby, 47–49
Pregnancy
  birth planning, 12–13
  care of mother, 10–11
  fetal stimulation, 5–6
  relaxation during, 3–4, 7–9, 14–16

R

Reading to baby, 112–114
Recipes
  food, 68–69, 96–98
  soap, 75–76
  See also Oil Treatments
Relaxation, prenatal, 3–4, 7–9, 14–16
Rice milk, 68

S

Savings accounts, 131–132
Scalp, baby's, 33–35
Schedules, 3–4, 29
Scrapbooks, 126–127
Self-esteem, building, 108–109
Self-feeding, 65, 95–98
Shampoos, homemade, 76
Siblings, 119, 128–129, 130
Sign language, 125
Skin lotions, 105–107
Sleep, of baby, 26, 73, 90–91
Slings, baby, 20–21, 88
Smell, sense of, 25–27
Soap, 75–76, 86
Socialization of baby, 118–119
Soft spot, 34, 116
Solid foods, 64–66, 67–69, 95–98
Songs
  for older babies, 101
  to build vocabulary, 125
  See also Music
Soy milk, 68
Special needs children, 120–121
Speech, 112–114, 124–125
Spoiling babies, 30

Other Storey Books
You Will Enjoy

Natural BabyCare, by Colleen K. Dodt. Using easy-to-follow instructions, you can make natural lotions, bath oils, creams, powders, and shampoos that will ensure glowing health and enhance the bond between parent and child. Includes information on self-care during pregnancy, infant massage, and gift ideas. 160 pages. Paperback. ISBN 0-88266-953-2.

Rosemary Gladstar's Herbal Remedies for Children's Health, by Rosemary Gladstar. Learn how popular and lesser known herbs have been used in different cultures to treat children's illnesses such as colic, fever, stomach distress, and even the common cold. Gladstar offers dozens of recipes for everything from herbal salves to tinctures to teas, plus dosage and storage guidelines. 80 pages. Paperback. ISBN 1-58017-153-2.

50 Simple Ways to Pamper Yourself, by Stephanie Tourles. Licensed esthetician Stephanie Tourles provides suggestions for relieving stress, promoting relaxation, and beautifying every part of the body. Contains recipes, tips, and techniques for giving your mind and body the care they deserve. 144 pages. Paperback. ISBN 1-58017-210-5.

The Essential Oils Book, by Colleen K. Dodt. A rich resource on the applications of aromatherapy and its uses in everyday life, including aromas for the home, business environments, and essences for friends and family. 160 pages. Paperback. ISBN 0-88266-913-3.

The Naturally Clean Home, by Karyn Siegel-Maier. You'll learn how to use the antiseptic and antiviral properties of herbs and essential oils in safer, more economical alternatives to commercial cleaning products for every room of the house. 160 pages. Paperback. ISBN 1-58017-194-X.

Making Herbal Dream Pillows, by Jim Long. Tuck a fragrant dream pillow into your pillowcase to promote tranquility, vivid dreams, relaxation, or creativity. This lavishly illustrated book offers step-by-step instructions for creating 15 herbal dream blends and pillows for custom-made dreams. 64 pages. Hardcover. ISBN 1-58017-075-5.

These books and other Storey books are available at your bookstore, farm store, garden center, or directly from Storey Books, Schoolhouse Road, Pownal, Vermont 05261, or by calling 1-800-441-5700. Or visit our Web site at www.storeybooks.com.